Intermediate Man

Intermediate Man

John Lachs

HACKETT PUBLISHING COMPANY

INDIANAPOLIS / CAMBRIDGE

For further information, please address
Hackett Publishing Company, Inc.
Box 55573, Indianapolis, Indiana 46205

Library of Congress Cataloging in Publication Data

Lachs, John.
    Intermediate man.

    1. Alienation (Social psychology)   2. Social structure.
3. Experience.   4. Influence (Psychology)
I. Title
HM291.L22   302.5   81-4806
ISBN 0-915145-12-X   AACR2

Contents

Acknowledgements

A number of people read earlier versions of this work. Their comments, in some cases extensive and detailed, helped me to make the book better than it would otherwise have been. I am particularly indebted to Glenn Erickson, George Kline, Douglas MacDonald, A. J. Mandt, John McDermott, Heinrich Meyer, Beth Singer, Henny Wenkart, my colleagues in the Philosophy Department at Vanderbilt University, and several nameless reviewers whose suggestions were mediated through the publisher.

Portions of earlier drafts of this book were published in *Theories of Alienation* (Geyer and Schweitzer, eds.; Nijhoff, 1976), *Ethics, Free Enterprise, and Public Policy* (DeGeorge and Pichler, eds.; Oxford, 1978), *Technology and Human Affairs* (Hickman and al-Hibri, eds.; Mosby, 1981), *The Personalist,* and *Anglican Theological Review.*

For my family...
three generations of immediacy

1 The Cost
Of Community

After the shipwreck, Robinson Crusoe lived alone on his Island of Despair for twenty-five years. He built his own house, made his own clothes, hunted, raised corn and milked his goats: he did everything necessary to sustain life and to satisfy it by himself. He had to make his own decisions concerning safety and the future; having made them he had to carry them out. Even the luxury of a comfortable adopted theology was denied him. His interpretation of the Bible and of his own condition, though conventional from the standpoint of the society that bred him, was spun with trouble out of his own brain.

Crusoe's existance, though impoverished in breadth and human contacts, nevertheless presents a picture of extraordinary richness and immediacy. He was in direct and intimate touch with the conditions of his existence. He knew all that was needed for life and he knew how to obtain it through his own efforts alone. No one did anything for him; the actions necessary to maintain his existence, express his personality and fulfill his life were all *his*. In this way, he made the island his own. On it he felt at.home far more than he had ever felt at home in York. He could appreciate its beauty, respect its seasons and live by its overwhelming, though largely creative power. His account of his stay there is framed in pride and tinged with a tender and sentimental love.

The arrival of Friday signalled the beginning of Crusoe's return to the comforts of human companionship. Some might insist that since man is essentially a social being, Crusoe's lonely existence stripped him of his humanity: his return to companionship was at once the return to a human life. There is no doubt some truth to this, though the magnitude of our ignorance of human nature makes it difficult to judge how much. At any rate, the blessings of society seemed so evident to Robinson Crusoe that he greeted the opportunity to resume even a minimal social life with great enthusiasm. Who would hesitate for a moment in his situation?

Yet the headlong rush for companionship is not all to the good. It may well be an indispensable condition of human life or even of life for humans, and its cost will seem insignificant to the lonely man. But the personal cost of social life increases with its complexity until, though perhaps still unavoidable, it can no longer be ignored.

There is both loss and gain in the advent of the second man. Each Friday brings his own Crusoe help and companionship. Work can now be split, resources pooled and strategies discussed. At the end of the day there is a satisfied hour to eat together and laugh, to relate all that befell us and boast a little of how we responded. There is also the shared enjoyment of the fruits of labor along with the special joy of seeing how as a result of our work the world is slowly changed to suit our will.

Since the contact between such individuals is cooperative and direct, tasks are likely to be apportioned by mutual agreement. There is, one might say, a direct contract between them: Crusoe offers protection and a share of the island, Friday pledges his labor. Much of what each does is done not only for himself but on behalf of the other, and on his behalf at his request. As a result each knows what the other attempts and accomplishes, and each views each action and every result, without difficulty, as his very own.

Some would argue that the inherent problem in such an arrangement is that of inequality. Marxists, for instance, maintain that the class to which a person belongs is centrally tied to the way in which he earns his living, to what he must do to eat and keep a home. Viewed in this light, the relation of Crusoe to Friday may well reveal a basic class distinction. The tasks they perform are not shared equally: Crusoe gives all the orders and reserves for his own

THE COST OF COMMUNITY

enjoyment all the better tasks. Friday's activities are, by contrast, menial and low. Crusoe thinks and Friday works the ground; he plots strategy while Friday keeps the watch.

The Marxist may well be right in this. Even the miniature society of these two men may not be exempt from the potential for destructive class struggle. The unequal division of tasks and the fact that Crusoe welcomed Friday to *his* island laid the ground-work for future conflicts of interest. The unequal distribution of activities may of course seem sensible in view of the unequal abilities of the agents. This would convince Plato, who thought that each should be given the tasks that suit him best. But, commit-ted to a different view of human nature, Marxists would not agree. Some recent psychologists and writers of utopias might argue that such inequality is justified if the parties to it embrace it happily. Strangely, perhaps, Marxists do not accept this, either. They believe that happy acceptance cannot annul the cost of some arrangements.

Is the main human cost of society, then, the unavoidable horror of class, exploitation and conflict of interest? And is the most fundamental social fact that of struggle to keep the other down? I think the answer is no. There is a more fundamental cost and a more fundamental fact. Marx himself agrees that it is possi-ble to have a society without class conflict. He goes so far as to say, in fact, that such a world, which he calls communist society, will necessarily come about. Class conflict, then, is neither inevitable nor universal.

The more fundamental fact I have in mind underlies the possibility of class conflict. It is present unavoidably, though to differing extents, in all societies. We find it in the rudimentary one of Crusoe and Friday no less than in a Marxist utopia. This fact is that of *mediation* or action on behalf of the other. Without our Fridays each of us would have to perform by himself all the actions that support his life and express his self. Our companions relieve us of many of these tasks. They interpose themselves between each person and those actions that would otherwise be his. Such inter-position is the essence of society and it would be shortsighted indeed to condemn it or to urge that it be quashed. At its best it is intelligent cooperation and shows that man can rise above the beasts.

The phenomenon of one's action being performed for one by another I shall call "the mediation of action." The person who performs the action on one's behalf is "the intermediate man": he stands between me and my action, making it impossible for me to experience it directly. He obstructs my view of the action and of its consequences alike. All of us have our actions mediated and all, in turn, are intermediate men.

The ubiquity of mediation has three major consequences. In performing our actions others become the instruments of our will. We tend to view such people as tools and to treat them as means to our ends. The first result, then, is the growing readiness to manipulate human beings, the tendency to regard people as desireless instruments for obtaining what we desire.

The second consequence is the growing sense of passivity and impotence that infects many of us. It is not that as more and more of our actions become mediated, we cease to do things ourselves. We may, in fact, be busier than ever, performing in a dozen social roles the mediated actions of others. But to do things is not to choose and act, to be busy is not to have the sense of personal accomplishment. What we lack is self-activity, the union in one person of aim, act and achievement, of motive and execution. Even Almighty God would feel a sense of impotence and frustration if, through self-limitation, He found it contingent on others that His will be done.

The third and perhaps most serious consequence of mediated action is the psychic distance it introduces between human beings and their actions. We quickly lose sight of the conditions of our existence and forget, if we ever knew, the immediate qualities and long-range effects of our actions. There appears to be something grotesque or paradoxical about a person failing to have direct experience of his actions. It conjures up the image of a man drunk or anaesthetized who can move through life without creating a ripple in his mind. We are clearly no such robots. Yet frequently we do not know what we work, nor how it feels to cause what we condone. It is not that our minds have shrunk through willful anaesthesia; instead, our bodies have grown larger or more numerous by the expansion of society and by the cementing of those structures and relations which enable us to act on each others' behalf. The responsibility for an act may be passed on, but its experience cannot. The result is that there are many acts no one consciously appropriates. For the person on whose behalf they are done, they exist only verbally or in the imagination: he will not claim them as his own since he never lived through them. The man who has actually done them, on the other hand, will always view them as someone else's and himself as but the blameless instrument of an alien will.

Psychic distance is a direct result of the lack of direct experience. It shows itself in our unwillingness or even inability to appropriate actions that are clearly ours. It is reinforced by the fact that intermediate men tend to hide from us the immediate and even many of the long-range consequences of our acts. Without firsthand acquaintance with his actions, even the best of humans moves in a moral vacuum: the abstract recognition of evil is neither a reliable guide nor an adequate motive. If we keep in mind the psychic distance between the agent and his act, along with its source in impoverished personal experience, we shall not be surprised at the immense and largely unintentional cruelty of men of good will. The mindless indifference of what is sometimes called "the system" is really our own indifference. It springs from our inability to appropriate acts as our own and thus assume responsibility for them. We do not know the suffering that is caused and cannot believe that *we* are the ones who cause it.

Our psychic distance from our deeds renders us ignorant of the conditions or our existence and the outcome of our acts. It fosters what seems to come naturally to most men anyway: blindness to the interconnection of all things, but especially of our acts and happiness. The distance we feel from our actions is proportionate to our ignorance of them; our ignorance, in turn, is largely a measure of the length of the chain of intermediaries between ourselves and our acts.

There is another factor involved in the growth of psychic distance. The longer and more extensive the chain of intermediaries, the less one retains control over them. As power over our actions and the indispensable conditions of our existence slips from our grasp, we begin to feel impotent and unimportant. The less we can regulate the intermediaries, the less we control their actions on our behalf. And the more we lose command of these actions, the more difficult it becomes to view them as our own. For a hundred years or more now we have known where this syndrome leads: inevitably we all end feeling helpless in an alien world. Drained of spontaneity, we move as in a dream or feel moved by an external, strange and overwhelming force. But for a hundred years or more we have supposed that the syndrome is the result of some malfunction in society. Views as to what malfunction differed widely: some thought it was the excess of struggle in society, others felt it was its paucity. Some convinced themselves that it was the existence of private property. Others claimed that it had to be the breakdown of community, of traditional authority or of hierarchical structure. No one seems to have taken seriously the idea that it is not a special feature of society that causes the sense of psychic distance, impotence and alienation among its members, but society itself. Yet if social life is a web of mediation and society a group of intermediate men, this conclusion appears inescapable. The productive question we must ask is not as to cause but antidote. If mediation and its deleterious results are present in each society, the problem is not how some special source begets them, but how some societies manage to counteract them at least in part.

An example might make the notions of mediation and psychic distance a little more concrete. The man left to his own devices to light his house with candle or with wick will learn a practical wisdom that comes only of direct contact with the world. At least within one sphere, he learns the operations of matter, the limits of human intervention and the cost in pain of every lumen shed. The same man living in an apartment complex in a large industrial society will progress little beyond knowledge of how to switch the light on and off. I thought it a breakthrough when, screwdriver in my uncertain hand, I peeked for the first time in the switching box. I have no quarrel with the benefits derived from the vast system of mediation institutionalized in the power companies. But consider the cost: public ignorance of the methods and costs of providing this central condition of public life, accompanied by defenseless dependence on an obscure though apparently reliable system. One part of the result is false security which, when destroyed, yields paralysis or a brutal response. And more pervasively, we have indifference to cost and consequence, which is the arrogance of blindness, not of power. The apartment dweller is agape but for a minute when he is told that what runs his lights also pollutes his air. Innocently, he backs up to his air conditioner and says, "But I can always clean my air by simply switching this on."

But, some might object, is mediation not just another name for the division of labor? I think it is not. Admittedly, there is a close connection between the two ideas. It is probable that when we act on each others' behalf, we perform divergent and perhaps complementary tasks. In our society, some govern, some educate and some raise corn. Conversely, when special limited tasks are assumed by individuals, it is probable that some, though not all, will perform acts aimed at benefiting others or relieving them of certain difficult burdens. Frequently, then, mediation takes the form of specialized labor performed for other persons. But mediation need not involve a division of tasks: it can occur between individuals all of whom are engaged in the same activity. Attorneys can represent other attorneys no less than they can act for retired Army engineers. And if this example fails to please, we can readily imagine a society of sustained mediation showing no division of labor at all. We may think, for example, of a religious community dedicated to self-humiliation and service in which each person meets the needs of just one other but none may ever act on his own behalf.

My first point, then, is that while the division of labor always involves mediation, the reverse is not true: mediation does not require that society contain specialist groups. We may thus view the division of labor as a special form of mediation or at least as a special way in which mediated chains may be constituted. It is, of course, by no means the only form or the only way: in subsequent chapters I shall show the presence of mediation in many activities (such as in the use of simple tools) where it is inappropriate to speak of a division of labor.

A second and perhaps more important point relates to the difference in orientation inherent in these concepts. The notion of a division of labor is social in character: it focuses attention on the role of groups, the relations of social strata or the activity of classes.

By contrast, the concept of mediation enables us to place activity where it rightfully belongs: on the level of the individual agent. This is not to deny the usefulness of analyses in terms of social groupings or economic interests. It is simply to reassert what seems so frequently forgotten: that all action, all consciousness and even all problems are ultimately the action, consciousness and problems of individuals. Mediation is, therefore, a concept that has immediate intuitive content and applicability for all of us. By employing it, I start from my own actions and how they relate to other persons and I always come back to see how their actions, in turn, affect my daily life.

One other objection appears obvious. Is not the general use of the notion of mediation dependent on an unreasonable extension of the idea of *my* action? Take the earlier case of the generation of electricity. Can we say more than that the people who work for the power companies provide a necessary service? Their actions are a means to my welfare and may even be an indispensable condition of my life. But why should we call them intermediaries standing betweed my and my acts? In what sense is the action of generating electricity, in which I am not actually, physically or directly involved, *mine?*

There is no easy general answer to the question of what it is that makes an act one's own. My physically performing an action will guarantee neither that it is mine nor that it is not. What is done by a man while suffering from total, though temporary, loss of memory will not in any important sense be his act. On the other hand, we do not hesitate to lay the blame for distant consequences on persons who did not commit the act. The man who hires a killer, for example, may be physically untainted, yet we think the murder is his doing.

The instance of the hired murderer is significant for at least two reasons. First, it shows that actions not directly performed by a person can yet be clearly his. Contracts, tacit and explicit, expand each person's agency as measured by our readiness to assign responsibility or praise and blame. Second, the case reminds us that sometimes there is an element of convention involved in deciding which action is whose. A full account of the causal antecedents of a given act will rarely if ever answer the question of whose it was. An additional factor involved is a convention, social practice or explicit decision about how far back we want to trace the causal chain or where we want to lodge the initial agency.

It is interesting to note how mediation, paradoxically, both contracts and expands our agency. On the one hand, few of the actions that sustain or fulfill my life are performed by me. They are done for me—many without my knowledge of what they are or why they are necessary. Yet, on the other hand, these actions are also mine, and mine not only because I would have had to do them or something like them, had there been no others to help out. For there is also a residual act or experience of the self that reveals the action as its own: we pay for services in kind or cash and bear, in any case, the natural consequences of what was done. My taxes and the bombs that fall on me affirm that my nation's acts of war are also mine. If there is anything to the idea of communal guilt, this surely is its conceptual foundation.

It is only by overlooking this interconnectedness of all agency that we can press the narrow question of whose exclusive property a given action is. To ask, "But whose is it really?" and perhaps to limit my acts to those I physically perform is to presuppose the fragmentation of agency typical of the mediated world. A broader perspective suggests that all the actions performed by members of a mediated chain belong to all its members. If actions belong to anyone, they are *ours*. This is one of the central facts awareness of which psychic distance suppresses. With ignorance of it goes ignorance of our social roots and fulfillment. And that, in turn makes it impossible for us to accept—even to see—our share of the responsibility for what there is and for what fails to be.

Of course, I do not mean that my nation's acts are mine no matter what I do. Nor are they mine simply because I benefit by them. They are my acts because I pay for them, not in money perhaps but in reciprocal services. Participants in a chain of mediation are united in mutuality. In making a contribution, each affirms support for the whole and acquires a share of the result. Through social relations we appropriate the act, even if psychic distance makes conscious embrace of it difficult. It is hollow to disclaim responsibility for slaughtered animals if we pay for a coat made of their skins or fur.

To see the conventional element involved in the claim that certain acts are mine, let us consider another case of mediation, one in which one's actions are performed by others far away and without one's detailed knowledge. I have in mind the institution and practices involved in representative government. The sheer size of our society makes the ideal of direct democracy, of the town meeting where each person can have his say, impractical. The next best thing to speaking for ourselves is to elect a person who will speak for us. The authority of the representative to act on our behalf, to act for us even to the extent of committing our funds and lives, derives from our authorizing him. As author of his own acts, each has a right to do certain things, though for or to himself alone; in electing a representative, we transfer some of our rights to him.

Note that the rights conferred are not narrowly specific. We do not send a man to Washington to vote for $10 more in Social Security payments and nothing else. We authorize him to act on our behalf without giving him specific limits or special instructions. There is hardly a law this side of the law of gravity he cannot vote to change; consequently, if his legislative colleagues cooperate, there is hardly a style of life or death he cannot choose for us. Yet, if there is anything to the idea of democratic self-government, we must believe that his actions are not only *means* to our welfare or indispensable conditions of our life. By conscious social decision we declare his actions ours and live as though the government's deeds embodied our will.

From this perspective, the question of whose property a given act really is does not admit of a simple, objectively true answer. What answer we can give is not discovered; it is something whose truth we help to create.

But such conventional ascriptions and appropriations of acts have psychological underpinnings. Some suppose that the political process of legitimating a government is sufficient to render the actions of the authorities *our* acts. Yet anyone caught on either side of a credibility gap or a revolution can testify that formal legitimation is neither necessary nor sufficient. Underlying the social institution of appropriating the acts of our representatives and setting limits to what they may do is the personal question, "Can we embrace their actions as our own?" The government's acts must be such as to enable citizens to *view* them as their own or at least not to view them as strange or unacceptable. In this sense, acts *are* our own if, but only if, we *see* them as and thus make them our own. When the community or a significant part of it ceases to view the actions of its representatives as its own, those representatives no longer have a legitimate claim to act on its behalf. The fragile bond of authority breaks: the government's acts are then no longer binding because those acts are no longer yours and mine.

We have, then, three different procedures by which we may conclude that an act is mine. The first is to trace social interactive patterns. Here acts I perform for others establish a partnership; I acquire a right to what they do, and a responsibility for it, by freely adding my contribution to the social structure or the needed product. These relationships are relatively unaffected by individual grasp of what goes on. Both the law and morality reflect this: ignorance of what one's employees did accidentally in error to another's home is no defense against the claim for reparations.

The second procedure is to follow social conventions. Physical and social interactive patterns are, of course, presupposed by such rules. But it is tradition and our purposes that determine where we lodge agency and responsibility for an act. Such social practices can change; when they do, persons hitherto guiltless find themselves in court.

The third procedure is to see whether the given act was or could be appropriated by me. Though such appropriation is primarily a matter of *viewing* the act as mine and of accepting its consequences, its limits are set by objective facts. In our society, at least, sincere but mistaken confession to a crime is not a ground for punishment. Yet many people do not think it at all strange for a person to offer assistance to American Indians as atonement for what his great-grandfather may have done to theirs.

In none of these three ways of ascribing acts does it involve an unnatural extension of meanings to say that an action not performed by me is, nevertheless, mine. The cooperative unity of the mediated world makes many distant actions unavoidably mine. But the psychic distance which attends mediation renders it difficult to appropriate them. Our social practices for lodging responsibility could reduce the growing gap between acts that are ours and those we appropriate. But these practices themselves lag behind the growth of mediation and rarely force us to assume responsibility for what unknown others do on our behalf.

Much of what I shall focus on by means of the concepts of mediation and psychic distance is traditionally thought to fall in the category of alienation. The classical literature on the subject leaves one with the impression that alienation is a single, simple concept. In fact, of course, this is clearly false. The notion of alienation has three major flaws. First of all, it is vague, lacking clear rules of application and a procedure by which we could determine which, if any, of its uses is correct. This leaves the referent of the concept substantially obscure.

Once we begin to specify the referent, we run into a second difficulty. The concept has been used rather indiscriminately to designate a variety of different conditions and circumstances. At the heart of this ambiguity is the inadequately appreciated difference between alienation as an objective condition of society or of individuals, and alienation as a subjectively experienced discomfort. And even within the general sphere of objective alienation, there has been a good deal of damaging confusion between alienation as a relation, as a process, and as a product.

The third flaw of the concept of alienation is its hybrid character. It is a notion used not only to describe but also to evaluate. It has descriptive force, in fact, only on condition of an antecedent and usually unrevealed moral judgment. This renders it virtually useless for purposes of objective communication. It is important to agree on the facts prior to judging them; if it is only the judgment that reveals the facts, we shall always be open to the charge of loading the dice and *creating* our evidence.

It is not, of course, that I shall refrain from making judgments. But I will not make them by simply calling an act mediated or declaring human relations to be characterized by psychic distance. For mediation and psychic distance are sometimes desirable and sometimes not, and whether they are or not depends on the context, on their consequences and on our needs. In themselves, they are describable conditions that obtain in society and in the soul. Some of their consequences clearly conduce to a better life. Others are costs. The advantage of these concepts over the idea of alienation is that through them descriptions and judgments become separable acts. And, while alienation seems an unmitigated evil, more realistically, mediation has both costs and benefits.

It is unlikely that we shall make much headway in understanding the source and nature of our social ailments without abandoning the idea of alienation. The concepts of mediation and psychic distance are prime candidates for replacing it: I hope to show that they can handle in an objective and accurate way all the phenomena which we now group under the alienation label. These concepts are clear, easily grasped and immediately applicable. They are essentially value-neutral and can thus provide the descriptive groundwork that must underlie responsible judgment.

The moral of Robinson Crusoe's condition is not that we should live in isolation from our fellows and do everything for ourselves. He is but a thought experiment, a limiting case designed to make a point. The point is that the more we are surrounded by intermediate men, the more we live in a cocoon of ignorance, passivity and sensory deprivation. Our horizon constricts and the world, now strange and distant, reports itself only through senseless rumblings or signals in unintelligible smoke.

The result is a loss of both self and world. Like some modern Jonah, we disappear in the belly of the great Leviathan of mediation. But Jonah had at least Jonah left, though in grievous condition. We have no private, active self, only some tasks, some roles and from time to time some fragmentary thoughts.

Community naturally leads to mediation and mediation to a loss of active self. We cannot rid ourselves of mediation. But we can counteract some of its worst effects. If we fail in this, as we have failed so far, the ultimate cost of community will be the impossibility of private fulfillment and public communion.

2 Machines That Shield Us

Some believe that it is never right to use another person as a means. Mediation that is thoroughly institutionalized hides much of this use and a great deal of exploitation. Yet the more steadfast among those of strong moral persuasion may never feel right about mediation unless it is limited to the use of non-rational and preferably even inanimate beings.

Such restriction, of course, entails the loss of civilization. It cannot even be conceived apart from artificially abstract circumstances of the sort under which Robinson Crusoe is imagined to exist. The great classical ideal of perfection, of which God was supposed to be the prime or only instance, is that of solitary independence, of having neither desires nor needs one cannot satisfy alone. Those who think we ought to get along without mediation by our fellows—without society—are tacitly committed to this ideal: they think that each man is somehow a god.

To be sure, mediation in the broadest sense does not require that the intermediary between the agent and his act be a person. The most rudimentary forms of mediation are in fact not human. The first involves the interposition of tools, in a broadly inclusive sense of the term, between oneself and one's action. This is the subject of the current chapter. In the second, our own actions serve as means or medium to our ends. I shall focus on this type of mediation in the following chapter.

By calling these forms of mediation rudimentary I do not

mean to imply that somehow they precede other forms or are more basic. My interest is not in some presumed sequence of development which, even if it ever occurred, is by now lost in the impenetrable haze that hides the history of early man. It is likely that every form of mediation is present in each society, though in each perhaps to a different extent. There is, of course, a growth in the complexity of societies, due partly at least to an increase in their size. But to arrange types of mediation in some easy-to-group sequence is not to reproduce their history, just as it is not to tell the story of a square to place it between a triangle and a pentagon.

My purpose is to see how many apparently diverse activities display the same pattern. I do this by attempting to bring disparate phenomena to the unity of a single idea. This must be done not only with caution but with a measure of rational scepticism. For in fitting facts to concepts there is always a bit of slippage and distortion. And, most important of all, there are alternative conceptualizations. An activity may appear as an autonomous fact on one view; on another, it may seem a truncated or extended form of others. In such matters a great deal depends on one's point of view. Depending on where we start, for example, the use of human beings to our ends may be viewed as a consequence or extension of our use of tools, or our use of tools may be considered a rudimentary form of human mediation. The question of which is the right starting point or correct perspective is misleading. The task is not to find the right concept but to gain a useful one. And usefulness is at least in part a matter of our purposes and goals.

Those who think of mind or consciousness as their essential self may view the body as a sullen tool. I want to start from a less controversial position. Picture a man driving nails with a hammer. There is no doubt that each act of pounding is uniquely his. On the face of it, therefore, he is not at a distance from his deeds. He knows his aim and feels his agency; he has little difficulty in appropriating every act. The easy exercise of his faculties, the quick succession of exertion and achievement may make his work a spontaneous delight.

It may seem, therefore, that tools do not hide the actions we perform by means of them, whereas human intermediaries normally do. And there appears to be an easy explanation for this:

tools are not self-motivating agents. Wherever we find them in operation the intentions and activities of the persons using them are never far behind. In brief, we do not think that our instruments do anything *for us*; rather, we think that *we do* things with them.

This view of the matter is, I think, false. It clearly has a point if we remain on the level of simple tools, such as the hammer, directly handled by a single person. But a large digital computer is also a tool, and it can readily hide the nature of the acts it performs on my behalf. And machines can loom even larger than that and seem more possessed of independent life. The plant manager or vice-president in charge of production has a momentous presence interposed between himself and his acts if his instrument is of the magnitude of an oil refinery, in which workers may be viewed as animate appendages of machines.

Psychic distance of some measure is bound to arise in all these cases. But it is there even in the instance of the simple, directly manipulated device. Imagine now that our friendly carpenter misses a nail and flattens his own finger. In a flash he discovers what it is like to the on the receiving end of his activity. To the reflective man this is not only a painful but a shocking realization. He simply did not know what force he was exerting in swinging his hammer. He may never have felt the effects of such force on a small, sensitive part of his body. He can suddenly see the hammer in his hand as a nightstick or a tool of medieval torture. The nails he hits might be human heads or breasts or fingernails shattered in their pink and trembling beds. In a rare flash of insight he might see how not suffering with the victim leads to cruelty. For though some atrocity is born of ill design, vastly more results of careless ignorance.

How can use of a simple instrument in plain view hide important aspects of our action? The key notion we must accept is that being in plain view is simply not enough. Each action has consequences in all sense modalities. To have anywhere near an adequate firsthand knowledge of it, we must experience it through several of our senses. Eyes, then, are not enough to convey full-bodied knowledge of an act simply because no single sense can be.

But there is more here than the general inadequacy of any one sense. For tools tend to take the place of our body in dealing with the world. They make it possible for us to act without coming in direct physical contact with what we act on, to affect objects and people even at a considerable remove. Though it takes the body to operate them, our instruments nonetheless shield us from exposure to the butt of action. There is a momentous difference between feeling a snake rub against one's leg and shooting lions at fifty yards.

All the experience of civilized man points in the direction of acting with dispatch and without involvement. We want to accomplish our ends not only with minimal physical effort but also with minimal bodily exposure. The clearest indication of this is the length to which we go to dress and protect the body, as if it were a weak or fragile object. Requirements of warmth, decency and convenience do not suffice to account for the use we make of boots and gloves and layer on layer of antiseptic clothing.

We work with tools in plain view and yet they hide the full reality of what we do. The reason is that the more we work with tools, the more we find that we have only a view. Bodily involvement culminating in physical touch is the most potent source of our sense of reality. Yet this is precisely what tools interdict. With the immediacy of physical encounter minimized and the immense emotional apparatus of touch detached, we can resort only to sight for information. And sight is a cool and impersonal medium: often it yields facts without feeling. The robust, multifaceted sense of reality fostered by direct physical engagement fades away. We become uninvolved observers of our deeds.

This suggests a neglected avenue of exploration in our search for the source of the dominance of sight in our lives. The use of tools, machines and man-made instruments, though involving physical acts, nonetheless reduces the exposure and hence the sensitivity of the body. This is what necessitates ever greater reliance on our eyes, while it progressively impoverishes our picture of what we cause.

Tools mediating our actions, then, have two general sorts of effects. They amplify our action on the world, increasing human might and versatility beyond anything a rational observer of our unreason could have predicted. But they also serve as a protective wall that cushions the impact of the world on us, dulls our senses and narrows direct experience. I have tried to show how these effects are present even the in the personal use in plain view of the simplest instruments. In an industrial society that places heavy reliance on man-made devices, the consequences become overwhelming.

The craftsman working with tools he understands can come to view them as extensions of his body. He can not only identify them as his, he can identify *with* them. Long experience with them teaches him their power and limits; occasional slips, which turn the tool on his body, render this knowledge vivid and immediate. As a result, though his knowledge is not all it could be, the craftsman can at least appropriate his tool-mediated acts. He can view them as his and bear the consequences.

This becomes largely impossible in our industrial world. The devices we use are too complex and too numerous for any one person to understand them. The system of machines on which we rely for continued life seems to be out of scale with our senses. Even those who operate the tools are largely in the dark as to their mode of action. The rest of us sink into comfortable ignorance of the conditions of our life. Such ignorance begins with no thought of these conditions and ends with the thought that there are none.

Our innocence of the operation of our world of tools is so widespread as to appear to be in no need of emphasis. Yet the magnitude of our ignorance of this ignorance demands that we not pass it by without a comment. We are like blissful and brainless fish swimming in an ocean of machinery. Our food and shelter are manufactured, our very air is polluted and purified by our instruments. Our bodies are built or crushed, our minds shaped by inanimate devices. We think that nothing but the possession and use of machines can give us respite or satisfaction. We fear that nothing can be done without artificial aid: for lack of microphones the human voice is stilled. We created and we operate the momentous machinery that undergirds civilized life, but it is not true that in any clear sense we are still in charge.

It is not, of course, that the instruments have acquired a mind of their own and are taking us to where their hearts desire. That is never the nature of true slavery. Our bondage is due to our desires. What makes us slaves to our machines is our ingenuous reliance on these means and our abject readiness to suit our ends to feasibility. Slavery is a comfortable state: if it were not pleasant, it would never be. It pays by providing what we want or need. What keeps us bound is not the force of threats but burning want, warm comfort and the habit of supporting a habit.

Mediating machines make for us a comfortable world of secondhand sensations. Wrapped in their cocoon we hear but distant rumbles in our dome of sleep.

I have tried to show that when we place tools as intermediaries between ourselves and the world, our knowledge even of our direct actions is naturally curtailed. As the tools become more complex and more numerous, we find firsthand experience in general retreat. At first only tactile contact is reduced. But when we turn to actions mediated by vastly complex machines, such as the car, or to those performed on our behalf by means of tools that others operate, such as the building of the car we shall later use, we encounter a general diminution, in each person's life, of knowledge by direct experience.

There are two interesting extensions of this effect. The first is that the specialization of instruments and facilities goes hand in hand with the specialization of persons. By appropriating sphere after sphere of activity as their exclusive domain, specialists render our lives ever more constricted and compartmentalized. This closes off whole regions of human experience to most of us. Birth and death, the great terminal events of human life, occur in special places hidden from our ken. Healing and destruction, creativity in the arts, and even opinion formation are normally beyond our reach: all are accomplished by trained and certified experts.

The second point is that as direct exposure to the world is curtailed in each of us, certain experiences tend altogether to drop out of the life of the human race. I do not have in mind here only the blatant or trivial cases, such as the experience of trying to make fire by striking stones. Though tools mediate our actions and reduce direct experience, there is a direct experience of operating with tools. As in the course of time certain sorts of tools fall into disuse, the skills required to operate them—the unique and sometimes beautiful experiences derived from working with them—all slowly disappear. No one hunts for lunch by tossing rocks at wild boar or a passing cow. There is some loss in this, no doubt. But the view that the gain does not outweigh it is confined to well-fed romantics who have never thrown a stone.

But these are not the only experiences the development of tools eliminates. There are many acts no one does and no one does for us; in the name of efficiency or convenience we have surrendered them to machines. There is hardly a cow milked by hand in the civilized world and no one participates in the communal hunt. The whole enterprise of providing food has, in fact, been so mechanized that one has to search far and wide for a man who has even a vestigial sense of the struggle with nature for sustenance. In the not too distant future we may face the day when none will remember how to sow or reap or what it is like to kill a sow to eat. Most of us know nothing about these experiences even now. Farms become factories and each meat-processing plant a total system, a huge black box with hogs marching in at one end while infinite links of sausage—"untouched by human hands"—hang at the other. This leaves ever more of us in ever more blissful ignorance of what it takes to keep us fed and fat.

One can imagine a child of the future standing in wonder, if wonder will survive, in front of one of these great engines of destruction and life, asking about the mysterious transformation of cow into canned meat. What could one say so he might understand? For this is not just a matter of pulleys and gears, of how parts of the machine interact. For him to understand we would have to explain what it is like to kill a dumb but harmless sentient beast in cold blood and for food. No explanation would ever suffice, of course: words cannot capture what the eyes and hands reveal. If the child could see the dim image of terror in those eyes, if he could sense with his whole body the death convulsions of the animal and then nonetheless sit to feed on it, he might spontaneously sense a sacramental element in eating or a deep unity with nature and her ways. Without these experiences the activity of eating remains meaningless and neutral: humans cease to be hungry animals and become empty tanks to be filled.

There are at least two other fundamental human experiences that are endangered by the spread of machines that mediate our contact with the world. The first is the experience of using the entirety of our bodies in the service of a task. The dog involves its body in the simplest acts: in joy all of its parts shriek happiness, in stalking even its hair attends. By contrast, we compartmentalize our acts: the hand doodles, the foot taps, the chin itches when we listen. The one act for which the total body is essential—carrying and balancing heavy weights, was first simplified by tools and then transferred to machines altogether. Now few of our normal tasks cause us to sweat; in the civilized world more sweat is due to worry than to work. Perhaps the only activities left that involve the whole body are sex, for those at least who do not view it as a localized sensation, and sport. Our devotion to them reflects a need for and joy in total involvement.

The second threat comes in an area dear to conservationists. As our machines spread, wilderness disappears. Yet there is something terribly important about encountering nature at first hand. The demand not to render species of animals extinct so that we may see them in their natural habitat is not frivolous. We are of nature and she lives in us. We claim not to know what ails us in the city, but is there no hint in the peace we find in the movement of a tree or in the passion of a squirrel in the park? Without continued contact with nature, without respect for the rhythm of her ways, we must forever feel without a home. We may choose not to live in her bosom, just as the child may choose to travel from its home. But perhaps we have to learn, as the child does, that to be too far away or to be barred from return by the mother's death is to lead a hopeless, homeless life.

Unaided human beings are relatively weak. The power our tools confer by amplifying our actions and the immunity they promise by protecting us have made us think that this is not really so. We act as if we believed that our strength and resources, even our lives, are limitless. We seem to think that everything can be done, that no natural process is immune to suspension or reversal by our might. All arrogance is ultimately arrogance of will. In its final form our arrogance shows itself as the belief that we can accomplish anything, if only we set our minds to it. Taken at face value this claim is simply false. As we grow up we learn with pain the limits of our talents and our time. There are similar limits for mankind, though as a race we seem to lack maturity to face them.

The illusion of our omnipotence leads us to disregard some simple and central facts about the world. The more we forget these facts the more our attitudes and actions reflect a false appraisal of our state and prospects. Before long we find our lives out of phase with the movements of the world; as our expectations become unreasonable, we feel never satisfied. The disregard of these facts leads to grave errors which plague us every day. What makes the errors dangerous is that they destroy even the possibility of happiness. What makes them remarkable is that if stated, they are easily exposed as fallacies: there is no intellect infirm enough to be fooled by them if they are plainly set in view. Yet we can live by such fallacies without knowing the error; they structure our lives and ruin them, and in our innocence we cannot find the culprit.

Let me call attention to two of these unspoken mistakes. Both grow directly out of our use of tools and man-made devices to mediate our acts. The first is our belief or hope that human actions are not attended by long-range and irreversible results. We might call this *the fallacy of avoidable consequences.* Since we have acquired a measure of control over nature, it is easy to suppose that we can always contravene her efficacy and reverse her habitual course. Our technology and much of our social life support the silent conviction that the natural consequences of our acts are optional and may at will be rescinded.

Pills and operations appear, to the casual observer, to go a long way toward undoing the ravages of nature. We routinely convert the damage wrought by catastrophes or culpable acts into the calculable medium of cash and feel that insurance payments cancel injuries. Our sense of the unstructured openness of the future makes it difficult for us to admit that we are bound by what we have been or done; this is at least a part of the reason for the instability of marriage in the modern world. For we think of human contacts and contracts not only as voluntary in their inception, but also as permanently terminable and tentative.

There is a young woman of my acquaintance, known for her eclectic taste in men, who has come to symbolize this error in my mind. She had had two abortions before she reached twenty. She was surprised, even indignant, when she became pregnant for the third time. She viewed her condition not as a natural result of her activities, but as a special calamity in need of explanation beyond what common sense or simple biology could provide. The same surprise and indignation were registered by the student who walked into my office to report that tests done on him had revealed permanent brain damage as a result of the protracted use of drugs. "What do I do now?" he asked in horror but still convinced that there was something he could do to make his problem simply disappear.

We do not seem to be able to accept that sometimes there is nothing we can do. Our acts have natural and inevitable effects. These are not always as spectacular and immediate as the spurt of blood from a severed toe; some of the most striking effects may at first grow in the dark, some of the most lasting ones may be delayed. But ineluctably the consequences return to haunt us. The moment comes when it is too late to clean our streams or to conserve oil. There is nothing we can do to change a mongoloid. And, above all, for all of us it is impossible to avoid deterioration and death. The attempt to save men from death by freezing their bodies until we find a cure for their sickness (or the secret of eternal life) is perhaps the most pathetic manifestation of this fallacy.

The fact is that even the pills we take and the devices we use to avoid the unwanted consequences of our actions have unwanted and unavoidable effects. The thalidomide disaster is but one instance of what I have in mind. From aspirin through birth control pills to morphine, the chemicals in our pharmacopeia are the source of much incidental harm. In counteracting the consequences of our actions we incur new consequences to counteract.

The second fallacy is connected with the first, though the two are not identical. The ease with which we shape the world with tools can make us think that success has no cost. Here, once again, the practices of our society contribute to a great extent to fostering this agreeable illusion. For much of the economy of our country rests on consumption that outstrips all reasonable need. We are caused to buy beyond our means by advertisers and retailers who encourage us to believe that the best of everything can be ours without effort and at once. When there is cost, it seems trivial by comparison with the benefit conferred: four or five dollars a day for a new car, a deodorant for success in business and romance, a subscription for lasting happiness. Everything seems easy: we can have or be whatever we want without sacrifice or loss or misery.

We might dub this the illusion of costless benefits or *the fallacy of free delight.* An animal fighting the hostile world alone rarely commits this blunder. For it, adversity must seem a law of nature and life a line of obstacles. If it has thoughts, it may view pain as the price it has to pay for pleasures and happiness as the return on suffering. Each new predicament might remind it that nothing worth having is either free or cheap, that the world always exacts a pound of flesh for an ounce of steak.

It must have been in response to such troubling thoughts that heaven, our boldest ideal, was conceived. There, at last, we can transcend the fatal balancing of loss and gain. To be sure, those fortunate enough to pass the Pearly Gates were supposed already to have paid the price, cheap as it would seem in retrospect, of eternal bliss. But, and this is the important thing, once entered on this blessed life the soul presumably reaps costless benefits. Exempt from desire and disease, freed of pain, need and loss, it can enjoy each rapture without the dark thought of a day of reckoning.

It is of such heaven on earth we dream when our thoughts are ruled by the fallacy of free delight. Mediation is so widespread in our world that the true cost of our acts and lives is hidden from our ken. Like the bugs that skate on the surface of uncharted waters or like denizens of a decadent court, we live deprived of the knowledge of what supports us. And should there be cost, we think our technical know-how will quickly erase the loss. Perhaps by next year we will achieve prevention and need no remedy. Hidden costs combined with the propaganda that there are really none, and the vast increase in power and reduction of effort made possible by machines, all further the creed that our pleasures are limitless and free.

The final stage in this trend has not yet arrived. It has been foreshadowed in technological utopias; reality suggests fiction to the receptive mind and then copies the fiction to make it all come true. The logic behind such utopias is Orwellian: if reason demands that we get the most for the least, is it not supremely rational to get everything for nothing or at least to feel that the world is ours, though we never paid? The strategy for accomplishing this has two parts. The first is the large-scale use of machines in production to minimize hard work and greatly to increase the availability of consumer goods. The second is the widespread application of psychological techniques. By their means people can be trained to dislike such costly goods as freedom and to love to bear the expense of all the rest. A cost we gladly pay will not appear to be a cost at all; in this way, we can actually come to believe that we lead a free and happy life.

This is what the Savage of *Brave New World* realizes in his intuitive and incoherent way. He senses that the society in which he finds himself is built on the fallacy of free delight, that there everyone is engineered to disregard costs or to suppose that there are none. People around him think they feel happy, though clearly none of them really is. The ultimate horror in his estimation is the shallowness of perpetual pleasure when measured against the surrender of free action and self-development, which is its cost. In this light, the Savage's otherwise puzzling or pathetic demand for the right to feel unhappy is suddenly revealed as the insistence on individual choice, which requires that costs be manifest. He thinks it ignominious to be duped into believing that all is well and free when in reality we pay for comfort with disfigured lives.

Motivating people to cooperate of their own accord, manipulating them from the inside, has always been the dream of tyrannies. Perhaps the only way to accomplish this is by creating the illusion that the government or the social structure it proposes will yield some great and costless benefits. Our technology and social practices antecedently incline us to believe that gratuitous gains are at least possible; in addition, we now have the psychological techniques to cause the conviction that a given regime actually provides such benefits. The ingredients, therefore, of a truly extensive and successful tyranny are already at hand.

In such a state, if it were ever to occur, citizens would love their government. Mediation would, of course, not be eliminated, nor would the psychic distance that flows from it be overcome. All questions of agency and responsibility would be submerged in institutionalized ignorance and ignorance would be concealed by pleasant feelings. The result could well be a generation of people who, without being happy, would feel as though they were and would never really know the difference.

But is there a difference? Perhaps nothing matters beyond how we feel, if our feelings could but be sustained. Synthetic happiness caused by machine, pill, propaganda or electrodes in the brain is preferable to none. Since it is the only type that can be guaranteed, perhaps it is better than any other. In the end, is liberty more than our sense that we are free? Is self-determination anything beyond the thought that we shape our destiny?

All of this sounds strangely plausible. Yet we find that the mere sense of satisfaction does not satisfy.

3 The Means Mediates

In an incident Aesop did not record, three animals were lamenting their fate. "If only I had more to eat," said the pig as he imagined himself buried under an avalanche of fragrant victuals. "If only I had shorter hours and less work," complained the ass as he rubbed his aching back. "If only people had more things and I greater skill to steal them," whispered the fox, for he did not want to be found out.

The God Zeus, known for his cruel sense of humor, heard their complaints and decided to grant the animals what they desired. The pig's larder was overflowing with food; he had so much that he had to ask the fox to store some of it for him. But soon the pig could no longer enjoy these good things. Eating too much had caused indigestion and now he could not stand the thought of cooking or of food. The ass's workday was reduced; his master bought a truck to do his heavy work. But soon, instead of attending to all the important things he had thought he would do, the ass fell asleep and spent his days in a stupor. The fox did not fall asleep. But once the initial glory of poaching chickens had abated, he grew indifferent to the charms of pillage. He was bored.

The fable will seem, of course, to have no moral for anyone who thinks that boredom, stupor and the glut that comes of overconsumption are integral parts of the happy life. In fact, however, many of us know that neither material plenty nor the instant fulfillment of our desires guarantees satisfaction. Improvements in the standard of living leave us more comfortable but not more happy. And, by a strange inversion, each granted wish makes us feel farther from wholeness and inner peace.

This did not appear so to the seventeenth-century English philosopher Thomas Hobbes, as it does not seem true to the official consciousness of the industrial world today. To Hobbes and to his soulmates in our midst, happiness is a function of the goods we possess and the things we consume: it is the result of urges satisfied. In his book, *Leviathan*, he expressed the idea in an eloquent definition:

> Continual success in obtaining those things which a man from time to time desires, that is to say, continual prospering, is what men call FELICITY.

If this is true, the introduction of massive advertising and of credit buying are the two greatest steps ever taken to promote the happiness of man. Advertisers create new desires and consumer credit makes it possible for these cravings to be instantly satisfied. The unbroken cycle of desires and satisfactions guaranteed amounts to that "continual prospering" which men call "felicity." Continual success, which is happiness, is the share of the American who desires, purchases and consumes in proportion to the installment payments he can meet. And it is plain that what is purchased need not be a fabricated object—it may be love. Nor must the payment be a sum of money—it may be time to listen to a woman's troubles or a promise of security.

Are Hobbes and his friends ultimately right that happiness is but the satisfaction of desires on the basis of wisdom in trading? If so, why do so many Americans, shrewd businessmen at work as well as in their private lives, remain unhappy? If Hobbes' analysis were correct, the use or consumption of physical objects and human emotions should suffice to make us happy. Why is it, then, that so many of us are successful as users and consumers of human feelings, yet judge ourselves unsuccessful as person and feel a deep and lasting insufficiency?

To begin to answer this question, we must note the extent to which the possession and use of manufactured physical objects

have become fundamental facts in our culture. They have pene-
trated even our thoughts: the attitudes appropriate to ownership
and use have come to serve as the model for our attitudes to the
world and to other human beings in it. Our attitude to almost
everything we have or wish for is that of a consumer. We use not
only cars, but also our reputation and the goodwill of our neighbors. We possess not only television sets, but also an education and
the loyalty of our friends.

It is, of course, natural for the human mind to reify the
intangible. We substitute images for attitudes and concrete objects
for abstract relations. But soon such conceptual aids cease to be
merely that. They invade our mental life and take charge of our
actions until we learn to treat human beings as physical objects
and to view human feelings as things to be consumed. The result is
that the good life becomes a life filled with goods, and our attempt
to live it culminates in a rage of possessiveness.

But this is only the beginning of an answer. For underlying
and supporting the attitudes of ownership and use is a whole
framework of mind which fosters preoccupation with instrumentalities. Our lives are taken up with the management of means.
Frequently these are not direct means to our ends but means to
further means, while achievement of our goals and enjoyment of
our achievements slowly fade from sight. For us the ownership of
objects is but a means to their use. Use, in turn, is the present
means to distant, future ends. The more worthwhile the goals, the
more difficult they seem; and difficulties throw us back to means.
We value human acts for what they bring and forget to praise them
for what they are. We deal in full barrels, yet rarely taste the
wine.

The current veneration of progress is an apt symptom of this
frame of mind. Progress is a kind of motion: it is motion in the
direction of some desirable goal. What differentiates it from mere
movement or aimless change is its directionality. Direction, in
turn, implies a point of reference: some state of affairs for which we
strive or an objective that is deemed worthwhile. We could well,
though I will not here, spend long in assailing the apologists of
progress on the issue of mistaken standards. For it is obvious that
some of the objectives in terms of which we measure our "pro-

gress" are altogether worthless. Perhaps only individuals can be improved and the idea of the general betterment of mankind is simply incoherent. But even if it is not, we cannot judge human advance by the increase of two-car families or of the consumption of electricity.

Instead of discussing standards, let me focus the issues by considering the scandalous slogan "Progress is our most important product." Progress in fact is a movement not a product, and its sole importance derives from the importance and the value of its goal. No progress is valuable in and of itself. Only its end is of any worth, and it is only by reference to this end that a change may be called progressive. The value of progressive change is, in this way, entirely derivative: it is wholly dependent on the value of the fixed objective at which progress aims.

This single reflection should eliminate the mistake of supposing that progress can or ought to go on indefinitely or, what comes to the same thing, that progress can be its own end. Like all forms of transit, progress aims at a destination, not at its own self-propagation. Its object is a state in which improvement ceases because its goal has been achieved. I am, of course, not denying that progress is a good thing in some sense of that ambiguous phrase. But good things are of two sorts. Some are desired for their own sake or as ends, others are wanted for what they yield or as means. Comfort and pleasure may be states we want in and of themselves; if so, they are valuable as *ends*. Given these ends, coal and power plants acquire value as *means*. They help in providing for our comfort and pleasure; though not intrinsically valuable, they are at least useful.

This is also true of progress. It may be useful but it is not intrinsically valuable. It is good as a means, but not as an end; it must have an end or objective other than itself. Thus progress can never be the goal of progress, and no advance can be indefinitely sustained. This last thought is particularly important to keep in mind at a time when rapid economic growth, which once seemed endless, begins at last to slow and by doing so causes a crisis in our values. The change we call progress, moreover, cannot take place without at least the possibility of fulfillment. And the more fervently we desire the attainment of our goal, the more we look forward to the time when progress, having got us our aim, will have ceased to be.

"Progress," therefore, is not a term of unqualified commendation. It denotes movement in the direction of that which does not yet exist, even though things would be better if it did: its existence implies a current lack, along with the hope of future consummation. For this reason, any society committed to progress is at once also committed to the future. And whoever is committed to the future tends to cease to live in the present. Yet it is impossible to live in anything but the present. The person who attempts to live in the future ends by not living at all: his present is saturated with impatience, a sense of worthlessness, a longing for the morrow. His concentration on what is yet to come blinds him to the satisfactions that are possible now. His desire to come closer to his goals makes his present a chamber of horrors. By hastening the passage of the days he wishes his life away. And not only his longing is agonized. After such fierce desire each attainment is an anticlimax. The object of desire when at last possessed is but a pale replica of what was to be. For unreleased emotion paints in hues reality can never match.

Meaning in life is not to be found in the future and the characteristically human malady of trying to find it there leads only to disappointment and despair. Caught between the incompleteness of striving and the essential insufficiency of the possessions which flow from desire and hard work, the future-directed man lives with a pervasive sense of anxiety and defeat. The symbol of this mode of existence, so widespread in our society, is the grotesque figure of the man who works so hard to provide for his retirement that he dies of a heart attack when he is forty-two.

My reference to the future-directed man as having a mode of *existence* is deliberate. In the commendatory sense of the word so familiar to all of us, he has nothing we can call a *life*. Life is more than surviving through the days. It must have elements of fulfillment and satisfaction. It must transcend the state of perpetual wish and permanent postponement. It cannot be a stretch of time, lit only by our efforts and our hope, through which we march, anaesthetized, to die.

Yet that is exactly what it seems to be if we spend our days endlessly devising means to distant ends. Paradoxically, what gets us nearer to our goals is also what keeps us forever at a distance. The means to what we want is always some action; yet the more our actions serve as only means, the more we lose our one sure source of joy. In an existence firmly guided by purposes, then, we find our actions interposed between our longing selves and what we want to be. The actions mediate our dreams and move us toward the objects of desire. But they also separate us from our true life, from the warmth and joy of immediate achievement and from the glow of spontaneity.

Two objections appear natural at this point. The first argues that such mediation is essential: without goals and the means which take us there, human existence could not be secure. Foresight and planning, work and even thought would seem to be impossible if we failed to fit acts to ends and to regiment our deeds. We cannot be birds that soar will-less in the wind.

This is surely true. I have as little interest in denying the facts as in overlooking their consequences. The fact that it is necessary to destroy or kill in order to eat does not exempt the practice from moral critique. The same holds true of mediation. Perhaps all forms of mediation are necessary or inevitable. My concern is not with how, if at all, they can be eliminated, but with understanding their nature and assessing their effects on our attempt to lead the good life. And there is little doubt that the cumulative effects of mediation throughout our society along with the special consequences of the practice of having our acts mediate our goals create powerful obstacles to satisfaction.

I have indicated before that persistent focus on the means tends to defer satisfaction and its attendant delight. The second objection maintains that this is not so. In fact, use or usefulness and enjoyment are perfectly compatible. The accumulation of money, for example, may well be a means to the satisfactions cash can buy. But it can also be a direct source of sustained pleasure: the process of making the money grow may itself give joy. And the same is true of spending our money. What is initially of interest only for the good results it brings can quickly come to have intrinsic value. At first we shop so we can meet our needs; now many take delight in simply shopping. There is, moreover, nothing in the way of combining these attitudes and enjoying both the process and its product.

Again, it would be futile to deny the facts. I shall not dispute that on occasion we can transform labored processes into pleasurable acts; on the contrary, I should like to urge that we do this more. But the fact that we can make a silk purse out of a sow's ear does not make the hog more elegant. The attitude of seeking fulfillment in the future and viewing each present act as means to later joys tends to destroy the natural satisfaction that attends the exercise of each of our parts. Once attention is shifted from the future and we begin to enjoy activities at the time we do them and for what they are, we have transcended the mentality that views life as a process of mediation toward distant ends. Our action may in fact create some later goods. But it is then not viewed as means to these: by a reversal, the goods are seen as its incidental bonus. The action is justified in its own terms and not by reference to some ulterior end. It is chosen for enjoyment and enjoyed as our choice. It is, in brief, not means to any end but an instrument of our self-expression.

The difference between being a *means* to some end and simply *causing* a result is one of intention. In viewing our acts as mediating means, we strip them of their worth and inner meaning. If we shift perspective and let the act be its own end, its efficacy is not at all impaired. It may still cause effects it would be good to have. If it does not, at least we have enjoyed the doing. And if it does, we will not think the act was worthless cost and the waiting for our goal a time of pain and longing.

That the crucial difference is one of focus or intention gives some support to the haunting though perhaps too optimistic view that happiness is always in our power. For it is only under the most extreme circumstances that there is nothing we can *do*. And normally it is quite within our power to regard our doings as so many ends. This could render each of our acts self-validating and joyous: each would shine with the light of a total crystal. We could then live in and through every one of our deeds, absorbed in the doing and satisfied in the accomplishment.

But as it is, our consciousness seems to be saturated not only with the haste and reslessness of perpetual process but also with the deep-seated conviction that means and end, process and product can never coincide. To suppose this is to commit a grave error. The heart of the mistake lies in the thought that our actions and their goals must be distinct and separated by time. The notion, therefore, of instantaneous achievement, of action in which effort and consummation are inseparably one, appears to us incoherent. Trained in delaying gratification and steeped in the ethic of hard work, we regard pleasant actions with a deep suspicion. We fear that what is easy or fun cannot be any good.

This error is a convenient starting point for refocusing our attention on some ancient and elementary wisdom. While we think of our acts and ends as distinct, our lives remain in unremitting process. A process is a sequence of actions or events, such as the reading of a newspaper. Each action in this series takes some time and derives its sense from the actions that precede and follow it. The aim of the process is to obtain information or at least to finish reading the article or the paper. In proceeding to accomplish this I read on line by line. The sum of all the lines read in succession constitutes the process; each line perused takes me closer to my goal.

But the goal is not achieved until every constituent action is performed. This reveals the essential incompleteness of all processes. For in a process the product or objective never coexists with the activity. The actions are in search of their goal but never find it until they have lapsed. Dynamic activity and desired state are, then, always separate. Even the elements of the process itself are variegated and presuppose each others' demise. I must cease reading the first line before I can start the next and all reading must be ended when at last the goal of having obtained all the information I need or of having read the paper is achieved. And what am I left with when the end is reached? With dead possessions: static information or the cold fact of simply having read.

The example of reading a newspaper is bland. But consider the applications of the idea of incomplete process. Almost every facet of our lives displays a process and can thus not be whole. Our best waking hours are spent earning a living. Yet while earning it we hardly feel alive. In getting to work and home and a thousand other necessary places we are in transit: some spend a sixth of their existence in their car. Yet every mile is poisoned with rush and the ceaseless wish to be where we are not. We scheme or bargain to control our friends; there is no end to the cunning we use to evoke the desired response even from strangers in business or in love. Yet manipulation is a constant longing, with uncertainty as its only sure result. We plan our whole existence saving for old age: enjoyment will come, we feel, when evening falls. Yet the dark wind snuffs out the evening candle or—and this is more lamentable—leaves us lusty but with toothless bite. Process always mediates our lives and rends them into bitter effort and belated achievement.

The idea which, if focused on, may help us escape this pervasive ratrace is that actions can be their own ends. Following Aristotle, I call such actions *activities*. Activities are always self-contained and satisfying, for in them the mediation of achievement through our acts ceases, and means and end are married in a single deed. In this way, we attain immediate contact with our goals. If my aim in reading is simply to read, if—as we are wont to say—I read "for enjoyment," I cannot fail to achieve that objective at every moment when my eyes scan print. And my satisfaction is instant and sustained when, instead of rushing to get somewhere, I walk just to be walking or for the joy it gives.

The fact that in doing what I do I have no ulterior goal in mind focuses my attention on the act. This focus is the basis for absorption. People engaged in activity typically take a self-forgetful stance: they act as if there were nothing but the act, as if even they themselves were only what they do. Such immersion in the act is the cornerstone of aesthetic enjoyment and religious—especially mystical—experience. But we find it more commonly in all of us when, instrumentalities transcended, consciousness settles in the immediate. All our innocent joys come of such activities. The businessman who wrests primary attention from next year's balance sheet and delights in the conduct of his affairs transforms the process of making money into enjoyable acts. The budding mechanic who tinkers with his car can convert bumbling frustration into carefree hours. Even the carpenter, whose end is the completed house, can disregard his ultimate objective and glory in the act of driving nails.

Activities may have a passive or an active source: passive, for instance, when we watch a film and active when we undertake to make one. But on a deeper level it is clear that each activity involves a positive exercise of our parts. The fear, therefore, that when we engage in activity, the lack of ulterior ends condemns us to decadence or torpor, is quite unjustified. If the cessation of progress spelled stagnation, no one would be more stagnant than the Christian God. For this God is usually conceived as free of desires and eternally unchanged. Yet for this very reason we also think of Him as ceaselessly and without a single unachieved purpose engaging in the highest activities. Activity, then, is not the sequestered sleep of the impotent: it is, instead, unfailing, instantaneous and enjoyable achievement.

I readily admit that all activity is intrinsically useless. This uselessness, however, is the best indication of its value. The useful merely produces good things without being one. Activity, on the other hand, is good in and of itself. Too often, our acts point beyond themselves like poisoned arrows. Too often, they are useful for bringing about ends that are worthless. Yet human activity can become its own reason for being. We can at least occasionally short-circuit the mediating function of our actions and enjoy immediacy with our goals. When this occurs our acts are valued but not for what they yield. This places them in the category of what is useless but, because of its intrinsic value, also priceless.

In one sense, of course, to engage in activity is to keep doing things without getting anywhere. But why should we wish to get somewhere if we are satisfied with whatever we are doing? Our everlasting restlessness betrays a dissatisfaction with what we have and what we do and what we are. Once we find something worth doing, it is reasonable to enjoy doing it and to ask for no more. If we are satisfied with what we do and are, it becomes unnecessary to look to the future and hope for improvement.

But perhaps we should not be satisfied, whatever our state. This sounds noble; yet we must ask at once in the name of what higher ideals we should sacrifice our happiness. There may be eloquent answers to this and their high emotion will convince a person or two. But most of us have little interest in being habitual malcontents or mad idealists. We would be happy to be happy, if only we could attain it easily and enjoy it in good conscience.

It is important to note that the transcendence of means-end

mentality has both limits and costs. First of all, in overcoming this form of mediation, we leave all other forms untouched. Moreover, attention to the rich immediacy of action is possible only from time to time. For some, the change of attitude required is too heroic to be a real option, and for nearly all, action that is its own end can be only the icing, not the cake. Immediacy cannot be a way of life: in the world acts lead to acts, consequences attend our deeds, and though our hearts may not be in the future, we must continue to frame purposes. If we do not, the cost is high and certain. Aesop's grasshopper could make carefree music at least through a summer; human life without foresight may fail instantly. And even if fortune favors it for a season, in the end absorption breeds dependency.

4 Intermediate Man: Person To Person

In Western movies the plot inevitably leads to the saloon. There the hero is challenged by the local bully or a hired gun. Knowing his strength and the righeousness of his cause, the clean young man at first declines. The unshaven antagonist persists, hurling insults, dripping venom, feigning contempt. The hero is controlled, but he is not a saint; a final slam at his mother or some other routinely revered female personage has him on his feet. The scene is set for the fiercest fisticuffs.

A showdown seems inevitable: the antagonists face each other with clenched intentions, ready to act. But suddenly a friend or foolish stranger finds himself, almost against his wish, between the straining giants. An arm against each, he stretches between them like the ocean that separates, yet by its central presence unites two continents. He acts as physical barrier and emotional salve. Presently the men cool a little; defiant, sulking or with a quiet curse, they sit down to a whiskey or to cards. The piano player starts a frantic tune and painted girls move in to cheer the customers: confrontation has been put off another day.

This central presence between warring camps yields a classic image of mediation. The peacemaker wedged in the middle is intermediate man. Like a lubricant injected between wearing metal parts, he reduces friction or cushions the impact of alien moves. This is done in the way mediation always works: by eliminating direct contact and thereby creating a distance between the agent and his object. In many cases such an artificial remove is genuinely useful, perhaps even indispensable for civilized conduct. The point of mediating conflicts by such presumably disinterested third parties as arbitrators, police officers and judges is at least in part to introduce cooling, if not healing, distance. Lawyers accomplish the same result routinely by assuming responsibility for all contact with the opposing side. The value of due process of law itself, in fact, is clearly tied to mediation. It is largely the consequence of two adroitly conceived distancing operations. The first separates the litigants and depersonalizes conflict by the introduction of disinterested intermediaries. The second produces, through slow-moving judicial machinery and elaborate procedures of appeal, a temporal lag between crime and its punishment or conflict and its resolution, and thereby creates ample time for resentments to cool and reason to prevail.

There is a risk, of course, to being in the middle, as anyone who ever gave advice in a marital squabble can quickly testify. The peacemaker may incur the united fury of antagonists. Hatred of the other side or burning love for it may be transferred to the middleman who pleads its cause until the personal complications of his charitable act make him curse the day he got involved. Alert friends, marital counselors and psychoanalysts take routine precautions to avoid this fate, though frequently their efforts are in vain.

In this chapter I shall not discuss courts and counselors or any other form of mediation that is institutionalized in our society. These will be the subject of the next chapter. Here I shall focus on mediation on the individual level. It is not always possible, of course, to draw a sharp distinction between the institutional and the individual. Family life, for instance, makes possible and on fortunate occasions includes some of the most direct and personal of human relations. Yet the family is an institution and it would be hopeless to try to determine how much of what happens in a home is the result of the way in which families are organized and operate in our society and how much is due to the idiosyncrasies of those who live there. Similarly, it may be impossible to decide which parts of our lives properly belong in or are products of the social history of our age and which are instances of true privacy.

But often when neat distinctions are hard to draw, they are hardly needed. What we need is to keep clearly in mind that the ground of the distinction is a difference in perspective and interests. However intimately the institutional and the individual may be intertwined, we can focus on the latter simply by adopting the standpoint of singular consciousness. That is my interest here: I want to see how the individual person encounters and experiences mediation. This is all the more important because individual consciousness is the only sort there is. Pleasure and happiness, suffering and horror are all focused here and made actual. What is not experienced in the throbbing mind of some conscious creature is never experienced at all; society bears fruit only in the felt fulfillment of the single person.

As we look at mediation from the perspective of personal experience, we can immediately distinguish two different types. The mediating agent in both is a person or group of persons. But in the one case he is wedged between two persons, in the other between a person and his acts. Our peacemaker in the Western saloon is an example of the first type. The second is typified by the men whom medieval kings and modern tyrants have on occasion employed to taste their food and test for lethal poison. Friday's relation to Robinson Crusoe was of this latter sort at first: he started by performing some of Crusoe's acts for him. When his master later used him to translate his orders to other natives, Friday began to act as a mediator of the former type. He then functioned as a man filling the gap between the parties, someone through whom the interaction of persons is achieved.

In both sorts of mediation there is an element of immediacy. We are in direct contact with the intermediary whether he merely does something on our behalf or represents us to somebody. But our interest is not in him; though he is our immediate contact, we look past him to what we want accomplished. He is an instrument of our will, prized not for who he is but for what he can do. Interest in him as a person arises only when his personality intrudes and he becomes unpredictable. Then we suddenly feel we must learn something about him to gain better control of his behavior. The more reliable the mediator, the more he is invisible as a person.

The individual whose acts he mediates would be glad to have him as a faceless cipher, if only his silent service never failed.

There are some conferences at which every speech is instantly translated into several languages. The bodiless voices that come over translation headphones there are such depersonalized mediators. One wonders how many United Nations delegates have ever met the owners of the voices whose quick translations they have heard for years. How many have even thought that there is a breathing, living person behind the nameless voice?

The myopia which disregards the personality of other persons appears an inevitable part of our lot. The cyclic requirements of life impose on us a round of daily tasks. Successful actions are universalized; the principle that the coup which works is always worth repeating governs our ceaseless search for the efficient and the easy. Soon we develop fixed modes of operation and our habits become sacred rituals. Life by its own momentum digs its groove and its channel; like a river, it sets limits to itself and builds the banks which confine it. Blindness is our inevitable state when, caught in silent iterative swirls, custom pulls us to the bottom of our lives. Then fading eyes lose sight of others or eyes intent on consequences look through those who are our instruments. Persons become invisible or transparent; to us they are only what they do.

I used to eat lunch in a student cafeteria where patrons had to clear their tables and pass their plates through a window to the dishwashing room. The opening, convenient to the hands, was just below the level of the eyes. One had to bend over a little to see the steam of the dishwasher and to realize that there were persons inside manning the machines. They were human beings with faces and feelings. They sweated in the heat of the machines and rarely talked; their life seemed completely absorbed in a single water ritual, in the endless baptism of unclean dishes. I spent six years collecting my plates and walking them to the window of these people before their presence and service rose to full consciousness in my mind. The hands must have reached out for my tray at least a thousand times. Yet I never saw them or never saw them as anything but moving objects in space. They must have seemed insignificant—perhaps parts of a machine, not the hands of persons who could smile.

Kant warned us of the immorality of treating others as means only. Yet the use of other persons and the attendant tendency to view them as manipulable tools are universal facts in our culture. Every culture is built on cooperative activity; this, in turn, provides benefits to each due to the efforts of all. Cooperation focuses attention on the act; the agents working with us are prized for their skills and their readiness to do what must be done. All of this is a natural process. To eliminate it is to eliminate its benefits, and no one can reasonably want that. Yet these benefits come at a high cost. The uniqueness, the internal feelings, the intrinsic value of those who do our bidding are disregarded. If human beings are tools, they are there to be used. If their sole or primary value is their use, they need not be conceived as having desires of their own; what we do for them is done not in response to their rights or needs or wants but in order to keep them in our service.

The result of all this is a consuming absorption with the means to manipulate our human tools. Communication becomes the art of control, the art of evoking desired consequences by saying, showing or doing. The feelings of others, their weaknesses and sensitivities themselves become exploitable features in the service of control. Advertising, public relations and the bulk of human interchange serve this manipulative function. In theological innocence we conceive that the role even of prayer is to obtain desired consequences: we think that by asking and thanking we are actually manipulating a susceptible Deity.

Use and exploitation, once they become habits, do not stop with others. Interest in our own intrinsic qualities, in the flowering of our own inner life becomes minimal. The focus on external results, on business in the broadest sense of the term, takes us beyond the inner landscape. Soon we learn to exploit our own infirmities in the service of our ends. Our educational system, no less than our system of rewards in business life, is designed to teach us to use ourselves to our advantage. Good students and good employees manipulate themselves by giving themselves rewards and punishments. They spend their life and energy freely for their goals, naively disregarding that their goals and satisfactions will lapse with waning life. There is no need to refute egotism beyond calling attention to our willing self-destruction by devotion to petty affairs and absorption in irrelevant business.

Perhaps we have never paid much attention to the internal landscape. The development of sensitivity, attention to sounds, colors and tastes for their own sake may be a late achievement in the history of man. In any case, they are frequently associated with decadence and the leisure that is the exclusive property of the well-to-do. Close attention to our emotions is itself normally considered sickly; the ideal is to pay no more attention to how we feel than is required for social adjustment.

The ultimate result is that we fail to treat even ourselves as ends. We disregard our intrinsically valuable experiences, or else convert them into mere signals of what goes on around us and indicators of what we ought to be. The intrinsic delight of the use of our senses breaks through on occasion: I once saw the busiest businessman transfixed by the smell of the lawn he had just mowed. He could not articulate what he sensed. There was a peculiar jumble of half-remembered thoughts and emotions in his heart, he later said. The simple, rich, all-pervasive fragrance blanked out his mind, destroyed for a moment his worries and his goals. For an eternal minute there was only the scent; he was his nostrils engulfing it until nothing was left but a drunkenness with life.

The fact that he later admitted he could not describe the scent beyond saying that it was the scent of new-mown grass is itself significant. Our language is focused on the world of external objects. We have no language for the inner life. Even our ability to discriminate internal phenomena is severely limited. I know people who cannot tell the difference between love and hate as these feel internally; they have to infer what their feelings are by observing themselves in action. Behaviorism and the theory of those who deny that we have "privileged" access to our inner states thus *come* true in our society: we render them true by closing the inner eye.

In the days when I was growing up, girls used to draw a careful distinction between loving a boy and merely liking him. I presume they consulted their feelings before they spoke. Students of classical languages fondly remind us that the ancient Greeks did even better: they were able to distinguish three different kinds of love. The love of God, of one's brother and of one's wife differ not only in their objects. This is perfectly clear from the fact that one can love the same person in three ways: one's wife, for instance, as a woman, as a human being ("sister," in the now common, extended sense of the word) and as a fellow creature of God. There is an internal difference in how one feels in each of these relationships. Lust shows itself in certain experiences in the chest and parts below; no one in his sane mind feels that way toward God.

But are there in fact only three sorts of phenomena we could call love? The differences in feeling from benign indifference to passionate devotion, from egotistic possessiveness to servile self-sacrifice are staggering in number and diversity. Words fail me, though my feelings do not; I know full well how I feel and how my feeling now differs from others like it, yet I am unable to say. This itself is a demonstration of my point, if it is not a personal failure, a shortcoming of my ability to describe. Yet I know it is not merely personal; even good poets feel more than they can say or make us feel.

We fail in the discrimination not only of our emotions, but also of our pains and pleasures and of the immediate objects of our senses. Physicians are continually beset by the difficulty of dealing with people who cannot tell where their bodies hurt and what form the pain takes. The English language is particularly impoverished when it comes to describing joy: what one experiences in winning at cards, in having an orgasm and in looking at a Kandinsky painting are all indifferently described as pleasure or enjoyment. And the very way in which we refer to smells and sounds and tactile sensations is infected with external reference. The scent the businessman experienced was the scent *of grass*. The taste sensation one has in eating a Yellow Delicious apple has its own special quality; yet all we can say about it is that it is the taste *of apple*. Modern music has detached sound from its characteristic functions and its sources, and modern painting has disjoined object and colors. Yet the liberation of the senses is far from complete: for the most part we still overlook the immediate features of the sensory experience in favor of the causal properties of the object we take it to reveal.

I dwell on our linguistic poverty at length because it reveals a poverty in our internal discriminations. And the poverty of our internal life, in turn, shuts us off from our most readily accessible and perhaps only experiences of intrinsic value. Lack of attention to the inner life is to a considerable extent self-caused. It is not wrought by deliberate design, but is a natural consequence of our overriding interest in manipulating others and ourselves. Plato remarked that thought was the dialogue of the soul with itself. Civilized life depends less on thought than on harnessed desire. In the end, therefore, civilization requires the manipulation of the soul by itself, the willing self-utilization of the self. We thus become means to our own ends, and this is on occasion called self-determination or freedom. Yet it may be important to remind ourselves that one can be a slave to oneself no less, and sometimes more inescapably, than one can be a slave to others.

Language is inadequate not only because it embodies an inadequate set of discriminations of our internal life. It can fulfill its communicative function only at a tremendous cost. Our psychic lives are richly overlaid with emotion: moments of consciousness are wet with anticipation and salty with memory. They are dipped in joy or sorrow, or else are saturated with palpable indifference. The language this rich brocade of emotive life generates, the language which describes or reports it is, by contrast, bland and dispassionate. Words hint at the passion seething below, but they always remain a cold medium.

The point is precisely that language acts as a medium; it is itself a mediating force. As such, it yields both the great benefits of mediation and also its unavoidable costs. Reflection, criticism and perhaps even self-knowledge are impossible without expression in a stable, relatively neutral medium. One can imagine a world in which persons communicated by telepathy. This might give them greater fellow-feeling and a more developed sense of human kinship and unity. But such a world would be conspicuously shy on planned cooperation, critical thought and the works of intellect.

Language is crucial, then, for human life. But it functions at the cost of a great loss in immediacy. The person to whom I attempt to convey my feelings gets but a pallid copy of what I live and breathe. The more accurate the description, in fact, the cooler it is, the less it engages the feelings. A precise, clinical description

53

of one's pain may be of scientific interest and intellectual value. But it has little immediacy: it does not motivate us to sense or feel or do. An inarticulate scream, by contrast, evokes alarm and sympathy. What it lacks in specificity it makes up for by the way it shakes us into empathetic action.

The sceptical doubts of philosophers about the possibility of communication are not whimsical or silly. They reside in legitimate worries we all have that people important to us will never know how we really feel. The worries focus on our feelings and private beliefs; these are the ones most difficult to convey. In communicating them through words or sounds or gestures we interpose an alien medium. Can we ever be sure that at the other end these words will cause the feelings that caused them?

Since we have nothing better, language in one form or another is the medium that unites our minds. Yet it also divides them, leaving the most classic of psychic gaps behind. By means of it we reach for one another, but when we touch, the hand we hold is gloved.

Language mediates not only our relation to each other, but also one's relation to oneself. Our access to ourselves is facilitated through the products of self-expression. How I feel or what I think about something is then best inferred from what I find myself saying about it. This, perhaps, is the technique of psychoanalysis: the patient is invited to speak freely and at length in the hope that his public words will reveal the hidden conflicts he would not allow himself to face in privacy. This trend culminates when even one's knowledge of oneself is word-mediated, so that I have to find out what I think of myself or who I think I am from scattered comments made to other people. This may in fact be a useful procedure; in any case, I would sooner know myself in this mediated way than not at all. But the more the method works, the less it becomes necessary to attend to ourselves firsthand. We then ignore direct access to our feelings, beliefs and personality. The inner life dries up and dies leaving us with an empty persona on the public stage.

In human interaction language functions both as mediator and as an instrument to overcome the effects of mediation. When persons act on each other's behalf, telling one another what they did and how may well be the most potent mediated way to remove psychic distance. Psychic distance is at its lowest ebb while social action is uniform, witnessed by all and restricted in scope. People do not feel distanced from the acts performed on their behalf by others if they themselves are performing similar acts at the same time. In the communal hunt of primitives we may have an instance of each acting for the others, and thus for himself, in unison; if each does essentially the same thing, each knows the action of everyone firsthand.

But mediation becomes genuinely useful only when the division of tasks in introduced, when varied skills are contributed to achieve a common end. Then the fastest in the tribe chase the animals to an appointed spot; there waiting spearsmen wound them to slow them down. Next, men with knives move in to finish the beasts and skin them. Finally, the women who have been watching all of this cook the meat in pots or salt and dry it. Here each group has a different task and hence undergoes a different experience. The women may not know what it is like to thrust the knife into a throbbing heart; the spearsmen may never know the exhilaration of a chase. But at least they share the experience as a whole: each is a witness to what the others do. The very fact that the entire operation is seen by all helps each to recognize and to respect his part in it. Each can truly say, "*We* killed the beast," and recall or imagine what was done as but a single social act. If there is any responsibility to be taken for the act, it will also be communal: if all jointly did what was performed, everyone is equally to praise.

In a case such as this, psychic distance is kept at a relative minimum. The reason is that each person actually sees everything or almost everything done. In watching, each vicariously enacts the moves of all, the way children mimic adults or a dozen troubled dogs stir in sympathy when they see two copulate. Remove visibility, the witnessing of each act by all, and you eliminate the sense of participation. The act may still be social, but it feels less so: the members of the group find it difficult to see how their contribution fits in. Send the women back to the village to tend the pots, have the spearsmen talk or smoke their pipes during the chase and the runners wander off or pull thorns from their toes once their task is done, and soon most of them are unable to tell what the others do or how the work of all can form a whole.

It is impractical even in a small tribe for things to come to a stop so everyone can watch everyone else do his thing in turn. In a complex industrial society, the very idea of this is absurd. We necessarily go off to do our thing out of sight of almost everyone else. Physical distance and sustained busyness rapidly increase the psychic distance between individuals. But soon it is not only lack of experience of what others do that separates us from their acts. Internal factors add their weight to these external ones: divergent tasks and skills make for different lives. What others do and what it means to them become first strange, then unintelligible, and finally altogether slip from view. The result is ignorance of the lives of others and hence also of how what they do is a condition of our own pleasure or survival.

Mediation is most useful when divergent persons contribute varied talents in the performance of different tasks. The growth of mediation of this sort is necessarily accompanied by the increase of psychic distance. As psychic distance increases, the sense of community tends to disappear. The hunting tribe still understands the importance of the contribution of each, the social nature of the process in which they engage and the relevance of it all to daily life and practice. This understanding has long lapsed by the time we reach our own way of feeding multitudes. The man on the assembly line at a soup factory finds the bulk of the complex process of which he is a minute part beyond the curvature of his horizon. He understands little of how chickens are raised or of the advantages of hydroponic tomatoes. He takes for granted the machine he works and the cans he fills; he knows next to nothing about marketing. He cannot guess, and perhaps he does not care to, why soup has to be cooked for as long and at just the temperature it is. His sole concern is to perform prescribed and sharply limited motions whose meaning he does not grasp.

The mailclerk at IBM, the accountant at Exxon, the middle-level executive at General Motors are all in this same position. The limits of their horizon may differ somewhat, but each understands considerably less than the totality of their corporation. They participate in but a few of the practices which render their firm a living, producing entity. And, of course, they have only a faint glimmer of the complex connections between businesses or of the staggering diversity of interrelated social acts.

Ignorance of the contribution of others and of the interconnectedness of the entire social fabric does more than impoverish the person. As the sense of community lapses, so does effective personal responsibility for social acts. Mediated individual acts have meaning only in their social context. As consciousness of the context drops out, the actions become unmeaning motions without consequence. With the consequences out of view, people can be parties to the most abhorrent acts without ever raising the question of their own role or responsibility. Wage earners who insert the fuse in bombs can then view their activity as but a series of repetitive motions performed for a living. Railroad workers who take trainloads of prisoners to exterminations camps can think of themselves as simply providing transportation. Some of their disclaimers of responsibility are admittedly what has aptly been called "preventive innocence": they want to make sure they are duly ordered to do their jobs and that they remain in ignorance of what it really is. We have seen a growing amount of such preventive innocence based on voluntary ignorance among people who occupy sensitive positions in government and industry. But more often than not, ignorance is not voluntary. The little man who claims to have been in the dark as to how his service aided social mischief may not be admired, but he must be respected for telling the truth.

How could persons who know little of the context and consequences of their acts be expected to assume responsibility for what they do? One's actions might form a minuscule partial cause of something much bigger which, when added to other distant causes, might lead to a condition with disastrous consequences. The planners themselves may not know the ultimate results. Even if they do, the masses of people used in achieving them certainly do not. Having no clear picture of how his actions relate to the operation of society, the average person feels blameless in imagined insularity.

The remarkable thing is that we are not unable to recognize wrong acts or gross injustices when we see them. What amazes us is how they could have come about when each of us did none but harmless acts. We look for someone to blame then, for conspiracies that might explain the horrors we all abhor. It is difficult to accept that often there is no person and no group that planned or caused it all. It is even more difficult to see how our own actions, through their remote effects, contributed to causing misery. It is no cop-out to think oneself blameless and condemn society. It is the natural result of large-scale mediation which inevitably leads to monstrous ignorance.

It is in combating this ignorance that language becomes a potent weapon against psychic distance. Through the mediation of words, actions can be put in their context. The distant consequences of what we do can be brought vividly before the mind. The flow of information by itself tends to make people more responsive and responsible. Moral philosophers through the ages may well have been wrong in thinking egotism the great bane of mankind. There are many selfish people, to be sure, and even more on ego-trips of near cosmic proportions. But there is more goodwill and basic decency among human beings than there is clear knowledge of what they really do. By knowledge, of course, I do not mean some abstract description of how bodies move. What we need most is understanding of the meaning of our acts, of how they connect with other events in the world and of what they cause.

The free flow of information about what we have wrought and what is being done on our behalf helps this understanding. Language is the natural medium in which such information gets disseminated. Yet, useful as language is, its efficacy is subject to sharp limitations. The connection between cold, descriptive language and action is itself weak and mediated. As a result, words tend not to engage us with the immediate force necessary to generate substantial response. The greatest immediacy is gained by full physical presence which opens all our senses. Immediate visual perception of a real situation is next most powerful; the power of the ears lags far behind. A further loss of impact is inevitable when what is seen or heard is itself of little moment: words must be transformed into ideas to acquire significance. The splendid gain in generality and cognitive power that accompanies this may far outweigh the loss in motive force, but that loss is very real, nonetheless.

The necessary translation of language into ideas sets an ultimate limit to the effectiveness of verbal interchange in a mediated world. Ideas do not grow like native berries in the mind. They are acquired by exposure to the real world. Language can, to some little extent, compensate for limited exposure. But on the whole, the limit of our ideas—at any rate of those ideas that are connected to our emotive and active parts—is the limit of our experience. As a result, men of divergent nature and differently circumscribed experience can understand but little about each other. Information about distant results and unexperienced consequences is not only abstract, it is actually unmeaning to many of us. We think we can understand it because our minds are carried by a phrase, as when we think we grasp what it is to possess a billion dollars. In fact, however, what we have is only rumor and fairy tale, a child's conception of the stars.

Language can be enlivened only by experience and common experience is precisely what mediation makes impossible. At least one unit of interaction in our society which, if properly used, might expand the sphere of common life is itself dying. The extended family used to provide experience of the most vital sort. It exhibited and taught the continuity of life. With three or four generations under the same roof, children learned tolerance for age and the old never felt useless, never lost their hope. United by anticipation and memory, vitality and repose joined hands in mutual acceptance, if not love. Mother and father could take comfort in being the link in this progression and everyone shared a silent understanding of his or her role in a natural cycle.

Families also provided firsthand acquaintance with a broad spectrum of skills. The father might be a locksmith, an uncle would cut hair, one of the grandfathers might have been a tailor way back when. All would cooperate in planting a garden in the spring; on summer evenings they swapped endless tales of love and early travels. There would be a maiden aunt about; grandmother knew all about medicines. Frequent visits from nearby relatives enlarged the child's horizon even more. He would try this and that and by the time he grew to be a man he had impressive skills and a fund of wisdom about the world.

By contrast, the nuclear family provides nothing like this.

Work around the house is a rushed necessity and work for wages is so repetitious and narrow that it presents little to discuss. The child is farmed out to school before his schooling starts: some have spent five years in pre-school and kindergarten by the time they enter the first grade. And in the schools teachers, themselves bereft of knowledge and experience, teach children through words what words can never teach. The result is the city child whose nearest experience of nature is the cockroach he encounters in the cracker-box. The nuclear family, especially as it exists in large cities, is unable to counteract the forces that pauperize experience. The shuffling of birth and death out of sight to safe special places where they occur under the supervision of experts is an outstanding example of what happens on a broader scale each day. Mediated man finds himself ignorant of natural sequences; the natural consequences of his acts appear to him in a distorted way or not at all.

Even a nuclear family could provide the opportunity to get to know at least one other person thoroughly. This may well be the one great benefit of childless monogamy. To get to know a person takes many years, perhaps a lifetime. The subtle dialectic of personal encounter framed in love is a deep and intrinsically fascinating experience. And the tenderness that comes of weaknesses accepted and shared memories seems at times the only thing that makes our lives attractive. Psychic distance could be at a minimum between husband and wife: the two of them could be as nearly one as two can be. Yet it rarely works out this way. The same absorption in externalities that leads attention away from the inner self also prompts the mate to ignore his alter-ego. Too often the husband views his wife as an instrument for house cleaning and sexual relief; the wife, by contrast, sees him as a meal ticket and a means to social respectability. Neither shows interest in the *person* of the other or in the interchange of thoughts and memories. They learn to live in the same house the way a squirrel and an owl live in a single tree, as independent agents sharing cordial neglect.

Those who insist on the liberation of women or on open marriage have little to propose that would enhance concern between the members of the partnership. They suggest that women engage in other independent activities than the ones they pursue now or in the same ones but with better conscience about the shared neglect. And when I say that their activities are independent, I do not mean simply that they are chosen by themselves. A high measure of self-determination is necessary for any successful marriage. But in many, independence of the parties means their readiness to make decisions without regard for the other. Self-determination shaped by care enhances love; without concern for what the other needs, it yields only resentment.

The family is, of course, not the only unit that can counteract the psychic distance naturally arising out of large-scale mediation. Education at its best has the same effect. The fact that education in our society does not fulfill this function is due in no small measure to the lack of recognition that this is a legitimate educational goal. The alternative to family life that has on occasion been attempted, involving dormitories for large numbers of like individuals performing similar tasks, does nothing toward reducing psychic distance. Dorms associated with factories or special projects, as we hear about these from China, leave little time for sharing thoughts at leisure. In any case, the experiences these workers could share are likely to be of a single texture, and it helps little to pool our ignorance.

In a world of mediation the individual finds himself as a single link in a long chain of structured interactions. He acts on behalf of others without knowing who those others are and how what he does helps them gain their ends. He is used as a tool, though frequently there is no central plan to use him. He, in turn, learns to rely on others and to expect that things will be done for him. On a personal level, this may take the form of manipulating those around him. More generally, his expectations show in his innocent readiness to take our world for granted.

The most fundamental cost of such mediation is growing ignorance. Experience of natural sequences becomes fragmented, understanding of the social nature of our acts decays. Psychologically, each person moves to an ever greater distance from the consequences of his actions and the conditions which make his existence possible. This growth of psychic distance makes it increasingly difficult for individuals to embrace, as their own, actions done on their behalf. Even those acts in which, in a minor sort of way, we participate, appear alien. The inability to see actions as our own naturally leads to reluctance and even incapacity to assume responsibility for them. At the same time, eager focus on our daily rounds, on manipulating others and ourselves, altogether blinds us to our self. Social irresponsibility, the impoverishment of our external vistas and the withering of our internal life, therefore, all proceed hand in hand propelled by the same developments.

We might think that this is the fate of the little man who is inescapably taped to the social organism. We might look with anticipation and envy at the position of the rich and the mighty, of those who lead or rule us. The saddest shock of all is to realize that there are no planners or controllers in our world of mediation: the leaders are no less the victims of psychic distance than we are.

5 Mediation Institutionalized

Cooperation on the basis of private agreement is one of the most intimate and satisfying of human relations. The motive for the contract may be selfish, yet the narrow bounds of the self are soon transcended. The sense of free self-determination in entering the arrangement is a source of quiet pleasure and there is exhilaration in sharing effort aimed at common goals. The mutuality in pleasing another and being pleased in turn makes free contract a high achievement—an ideal, some claim, as exalted as human nature will allow.

At its best, what some consider the sordidness in contracts— that we do things only in return for what others do for us—drops out. The exchange of goods or services then seems natural: it feels like a case of sharing, not of trading. The lived contract of marriage is sometimes like this, and this probably is also how Friday and Crusoe got along. The contract is no written instrument that is enforceable and therefore threatening. It is the lived cooperative practice of the parties based on habits developed, not on resolutions backed by force or law.

The contract ties two individuals together in the pursuit of one goal. If it is made consciously, it might require an adjustment of costs to benefits; this is what bargaining is all about. Bargaining is an intensely personal encounter. It reveals the individual and his values better than virtually anything short of a threat to life. No one play-acts in bargaining, none does it calmly on his own account as if the result did not matter. Emotions enter almost at once, feelings and commitments crowd in to obscure clear vision. The street vendor outside the Uffizi Palace in Florence arguing over a leather purse finds himself totally involved: every atom in his anatomy is intent on keeping the price as high as is consistent with keeping his customer.

We might instructively compare with this personal encounter, which leaves the client limp with exhaustion whether he wins or loses, the bland experience of contracting for electrical service. Let there be no mistake about this: the average person has much more at stake in such continuing contract for essential service than in the purchase of any trivial goods. Yet there is no bargaining and there is no personal encounter as the contract is made. A bored clerk hands over papers, one signs and writes a check; that is all there is to it. Although both clerk and customer are persons, the contract they execute is not personal. Each acts in a role that is routinized and stripped of individuality. Either one could be a computer terminal and nothing would be changed. The attempt to smile or to joke or in some other timid way to make the relationship less formal is quickly rebuffed. If a joke is successful, you might share a laugh, even if only in the way water and land share distant thunder. Then, if the clerk is of the opposite sex, you might make a date for the weekend. But frequently even this fails to make he relation personal: in our world commercial roles and sex roles are of the same fabric. In connecting them neither is transcended.

The key, of course, is that the clerk does not make the contract for himself. He is not a contracting party, but only acts for one. Children alone overlook this, even though the rest of us are no less naive about the consequences of such mediation. I remember a book my children once enjoyed about a "Milkman Bill." Little Dan falls ill and makes friends with the milkman who, he innocently thinks, actually milks the cows or even owns them. Bill arranges a tour of the plant for Dan, but it soon turns out that he does not know enough to conduct it. The boy is handed over to a manager who shows him trucks and vats and the pasteurizing process. In his excitement Dan does not notice that what he learns the milkman does not know. What would the boy think of his hero if he realized that Milkman Bill had in all probability never seen a cow? Though to Dan the milkman *is* the milk company, to Bill being a milkman is just a delivery job.

There are two way in which mediation gets institutionalized. The first develops as a result of the recognition that in many circumstances shared specialized labor is particularly useful. In some cases it may be the only way to accomplish the task. And in certain situations there is a special value to interposing persons between warring or rival parties. This is routinized and before long we have special occupations whose sole task is to mediate between people. By institutionalizing shared specialized labor we get the complex manufacturing processes of industrial civilization. By institutionalizing special intermediaries between separate parties we get the profession of law, professional arbitrators and the police in some of their roles. Such intermediaries are of value not only between individuals or groups in conflict. Sometimes their role is to bridge the gap between groups that would otherwise not be connected: this is the role of the middleman in commerce.

The second way in which mediation is institutionalized presupposes the first. Institutions are but complex patterns of human interaction; their very development is predicated on persons assuming specialized roles in which they act on behalf of one another. When these institutions are developed, they begin to acquire a reality and a personality of their own. The more complex mediation I have in mind occurs when officeholders in institutions no longer act on behalf of any one or group of individuals. At a certain stage, reality takes on a new complexion and this is reflected in our language. We find the company president saying that *General Motors* will pay a higher dividend this year. And the Board of TVA announces (not a person on behalf of TVA, but an impersonal board which, as reflected by the third person singular of the verb it takes, is nonetheless conceived as a unitary entity) that *TVA* will build six nuclear power plants in the next ten years. Even on the level of government there has been a substantial change. Originally, the lands in America were claimed by Columbus on behalf of Her Majesty Queen Isabella. For a while, lands were taken from the Indians for "the people of the United States." By the time we reached the moon, however, the claim laid to it, or to as much of it as we can keep to ourselves, was by *The United States*, as though that were a real being.

In acting in a role within an institution, we act on behalf of the institution directly, and only indirectly on behalf of the individuals whom that institution serves. We mediate, then, not the actions of persons but the "actions" of a mediated complex. The result is the fiction that such mediated complexes can act, that institutions are somehow real and perhaps even more real than persons. Corporations begin to appear as animate beings, as creatures with a soul, and we find ourselves asking in total seriousness about the social responsibility of businesses.

We would never dream of thinking that a dog or an ape is a morally responsible agent. Yet we unhesitatingly praise and blame corporations for what they do or fail to do. We clearly think of them as endowed with the deliberative and executive powers of a person. We can even punish them in the way we punish persons, by deliberately inflicting undesirable consequences on them. We can fine them and restrict their freedom of operation—punishments identical or analogous to those visited upon individuals.

Sociologists, who attack all abstractions not their own, apparently see no problem in endowing institutions with agency and personality. Even Marxists take pleasure in blaming corporations or "the prevailing social arrangements" for whatever evils they can detect in society. The culmination of this unfortunate tendency to view institutions as agencies is the Hegelian belief that the state is the most real of organisms and that individual fulfillment can come, therefore, only as a result of integrating oneself into the great Leviathan. If this were true, our obligations would be circumscribed by the laws and the tasks imposed on us by our social position and roles.

The fiction that institutions are efficacious agencies could have been created and can hold us spellbound only because of the universality of mediation. First of all, there can be no institutions without mediated human activity, without people performing divergent tasks on each others' behalf. Second, it is only the psychic distance attendant on widespread mediation that makes it possible for us to forget that ultimate agency always resides in the individual. The curvature of our horizon is such that almost everything but the roles we and others play falls below it. It is not persons we see, nor do we view their interactions as traceable patterns of mediation. We see only disconnected roles and if we do not assign independent rationality to the underlying institution, we cannot explain how they are connected. Our focus on people exclusively from the perspective of the slots they fill distances us from living persons. As a result, we view their behavior as governed by social rules or as required by their roles. This endows rules and roles with what appears to be magical power. We never ask about, much less understand, the tendencies and affections of the individual through which and through which alone rules and roles can achieve efficacy.

What is at stake here is a radical divergence in perspective. To assign efficacy to institutions is like thinking of the concepts and laws of geometry as active. In a terribly superficial way, one could view buildings as being made of rectangles, triangles, squares and other plane figures. That is the way it seems, if we confine ourselves to the medium of pure sight. But there is no end to the bafflement to which such narrow phenomenalism leads. It may be a consistent view, but it is too narrow. One has to go to outlandish excesses to explain how plane figures can accomplish all the things they apparently did. The more natural perspective is the one we still hold, at least concerning how buildings are built. Plane figures do nothing; ideas of them occur to flesh and blood persons with needs and purposes. Certain shapes seem attractive to these people and they incorporate them in the design of their homes.

Similarly, rules and roles, corporations and institutions have no efficacy whatever. To think that they do is due to a radically superficial perspective. Once we move below the surface we understand that the right questions to ask are not concerning how institutions generate or rules shape behavior. Instead, we have to inquire into why people with the needs and purposes and social history they have behave in accordance with certain rules and find certain institutions, though not others, fulfilling or natural. It is people who embrace customs and perpetuate them, not customs which find or generate groups for their own embodiment. It is people who create institutions, albeit frequently without design or foresight, not institutions that work for their own realization or perpetuation. Mediation blinds us to the personality as well as the agency of the person. As a result, we do not ask organic questions about the person, the being who lives by the rules and unites in himself (or else fails to) all the roles which he assumes. In a mediated world the individual agent is at an infinite psychic distance; since nothing gets done without some agency, we make inanimate institutions take his place.

The tendency to view institutions as real agents is unfortunate for at least two reasons. First of all, the more we think of governments and corporations as giant organisms, the more we feel helpless and passive in their presence. We feel victimized by superhuman powers and soon learn to attribute all our misfortunes to "the system." Admittedly, this is at least partly an excuse for personal indolence. But there is also an element of gripping honesty to it: we really do feel impotent when confronted by big government, big labor and big business. And the more we feel impotent, the more impotent we become. There really is an element of powerlessness which aggravates our plight, yet it is not that we lack power because our institutions have it all. Quite to the contrary: institutions have none and we have a little. The problem is that any single individual has very little, precisely because there are so many individuals and because chains of mediation become uncontrollable in direct proportion to their size.

Second, the more we think of states and corporations as endowed with moral personality, the more morality vanishes from the scene. For the reassignment of agency to the corporation gives moral agents a perfect excuse. Each can declare that he is working for the good of the whole or at the command of superiors. Each can convince himself that he is a victim of circumstance, an insignificant cog in the machine. How can anyone be held responsible if he is not an autonomous source of activity, if agency, so to speak, merely flows through him the way it flows through each link in a metal chain?

Responsibility is inconsistent with anonymity. Yet links in a chain of mediation have no names and no personality. All that is caught of the man is the role he plays, the job he performs; he is mimeograph clerk, concentration camp guard or the sergeant assigned to command an execution squad. The man is uninvolved in the job: job-activity is combined with personal passivity. Hence one does not, and perhaps cannot, see one's action as one's own. One can then effectively hide behind one's role: I cannot be expected to assume responsibility for what as an individual I did not do. This abnegation of personality naturally leads to the ultimate cop-out. The man cornered by his conscience can at some point no longer avoid knowing that what his role requires him to do is wrong. He then justifies his act by the final shriek of impotence: "If I did not do it, they would simply get somebody else," he says and feels satisfied for a moment as a helpless agent of the unavoidable.

Much of modern society is run by the sort of committee mentality I have described. There is safety and convenience in this. One can have one's say in the committee, one can pull one's weight in the institution simply by following the rules, without the need for much moral reflection and without the danger of being singled out as the person accountable. But it is important to ask why we need and seek the security of moral namelessness. The person who cannot be blamed cannot be praised either. Our normal tendency is to seek praise and not the indifference accorded to walls and furniture. We give up the hope of praise precisely because the probability of blame is too high. The chains of mediation in which we are involved are difficult to understand and impossible to control. Our half-conscious decision is to surrender possible praise for what we did to avoid probable blame for what uncontrolled others make it yield.

As institutionalized mediation grows, personal control over social acts and personal responsibility for them wane together. It is not that social life is without regularity or intelligible pattern. But the pattern is no more than the repetition of the similar under similar circumstances. It is not an achievement due to design and careful planning. There is an element of drift in the life of even the most rigidly controlled society and this drift is due to the inherent inability of centrally placed agents to control what goes on at the periphery. The slippage has been present in all empires, no matter how well run. The Emperor of Rome had little control over what went on in the provinces. While Genghis Khan raided Europe, his desires were chronically disregarded, misrepresented or misinterpreted back home. Even in Stalin's Russia, commissars had to be removed repeatedly to assure closer compliance with government decrees.

A tragic case of such slippage occurred during the Second World War in the Philippines, where the Japanese General Tomoyuki Yamashita ordered his troops to do what was necessary to stop guerrilla activity. It may be reasonable to believe, as he argued at his subsequent war crimes trial, that he did not mean for the troops to commit atrocities and would have stopped them had he known what they were doing. The fact is that in spite of all the paraphernalia of modern communication, he was not in effective control of his troops, just as decades later American commanders—with even better equipment—were apparently not in effective control at the time of the My Lai massacre in Vietnam. The loss of control is a direct consequence of mediation. Its magnitude varies with the number of intermediaries involved (the chain of command) and the distance, both physical and psychological, at which policies are executed.

The physical distance can to some extent be overcome by radio and telephone and television. Since it is a function of mediation, the psychological distance is more difficult to handle. For the instruments of communication, though they bring us closer to one another, do so only through extensive mediated chains. By using them we gain a truncated, incomplete immediacy. To minimize the likelihood of abuse, Yamashita should have known his officers. He should have had firsthand experience from the perspective of his foot soldiers of dealing with Philippine villagers and of moving for tense and frustrating days in a hostile jungle. Short of this he could never have understood how an order that to him seemed professional and innocent could have been interpreted as a license for torture. The state of mind of the soldier on the line was infinitely distant from General Yamashita's intentions and understanding; without shared experience the center cannot hold. With the best will all around, the person who executes the directive may become an executioner.

The War Crimes Tribunal understood all of this, but refused

to accept the claim that as control slips responsibility diminishes. Yamashita was convicted and put to death on the assumption that as initiator of a chain of mediation, he was accountable for what happened all the way down the line. One can understand the sense of unfairness this verdict must have engendered in the General's heart. He must have known that the court was making an example of him. Persons lodged in the center of mediated chains elsewhere experienced the same slippage and unwittingly caused lamentable consequences of the same sort, if not of the same magnitude, yet it would not occur to anyone to hold them responsible. The agency of one man simply does not extend that far, Yamashita must have felt. He was, of course, right in this. His agency did not extend so far as to be able to control his men. His intentions were honorable; he was a victim of circumstance. Yet the court's verdict was strikingly wise in giving him not what he in fact deserved by current social norms, but what he ought to have got if there was to be justice in the world. For one way to read the decision is as an attempt to create new norms: to expand the scope of our notion of responsibility, to revise the practice of identifying the agent in social acts, and to eliminate certain excusing conditions, all in order to bring law more closely in line with the reality of mediation.

The court's decree is notable because of its refusal to accept moral namelessness. Both Yamashita and his soldiers had what might seem to the world a valid excuse. Each side could point to the other: the soldiers could claim that they were ordered to do what they did, while their general could self-righteously maintain that his intentions were innocent and trouble came only because they were misread. The situation was not unlike one Steinbeck describes in *The Grapes of Wrath*. The men who come to evict farmers from their land seem to the victims as the enemy. Yet they claim innocence: they have been sent by the bank, they are only doing their job. If they did not act faithfully on behalf of their employers or if they were shot, others—perhaps far worse than themselves—would be hired to take their place. The local banker himself is not to blame. He has his bills to pay and takes *his* orders from others far away. And those far away are, presumably, in the same bind. No one means ill, everyone is caught; we are all innocent parties to an agentless crime. The desperate farmers go straight to the heart of the matter. If all of this is so, they ask, then whom do we shoot?

The War Crimes Tribunal's answer to this is that you shoot (or hang) the man who is at the center of the chain of mediation. To do so is to reject the claim that the loss of control entitles us to disclaim responsibility. From the standpoint of the classic maxim of moral philosophy that one is obliged to do only what one can, Yamashita was blameless. Given his circumstances, the social practices in the midst of which he found himself, his education, and his past experience, it was simply not within his power to control what went on in the field. The court's verdict is so striking because it simply disregards this very real inability: it says, in effect, that he should have controlled his troops, whether he was able to or not. He should have put himself in a position where he could control them, or else suffer for their misdeeds as though they were his own. The message to all of us is that acts done at our behest, no matter at what distance and however much at odds with our intentions, are ours; that mediation will not be allowed to destroy the gossamer fabric of responsibility. The court did not convict on the basis of existing norms of morality; it boldly engaged in the enterprise of creating more stringent standards.

But the War Crimes Tribunal evidently did not go far enough. We are left with a sense of injustice in seeing the initiator punished while the executioner goes free. In the My Lai incident, which is in many respects similar to the Japanese massacres in the Philippines, we are left with an equal sense of injustice, but for the opposite reason. For there the military court punished the immediate perpetrator without making a serious effort to bring his superiors to account. In point of fact, to create new standards of assigning responsibility we must collapse the chain of mediation in two directions at once. Those far from the action-end of mediated chains must be made to understand that their distance from the ultimate agents and consequences does not protect them from accountability. And those who execute orders must be impressed with the painful fact that mindlessly following directives or allowing what is construed as the causal force of society to flow through one is no sure foundation of innocence. Soldiers and all the rest of us at the active end of mediated chains must learn that there are some acts in which we must simply not participate.

These are hard lesssons to learn. Mediated chains direct attention away from the immediate. What is before us comes to be taken as a signal of what is far away and the full impact of what assaults our senses is cushioned by a hundred second thoughts. By a strange inversion, the abstract, the faceless and the invisible then become more real than the realities we bump into and the objects we love or eat. This is how we become organization men, devoted to country, church and corporation more than we are devoted to the persons these institutions serve. The abstract acquires such frightful force in our minds that when our faceless institution calls, all good sense and human decency are forgotten. We can delight in the smell of burning flesh if those burned are heretics; we can starve or kill children because they are children of the enemy; we gladly cause the financial and personal ruin of our competition.

We are not full of the milk of human kindness and it is unlikely that we would be filled by it, like empty glasses, at once if only mediation were overcome. Human nature, at least in the form we know it in others and live it in ourselves, is a peculiar amalgam of cruelty and good feeling. The wickedness that flows from impulse or design is commonplace and should never surprise. But there is also something akin to spontaneous sympathy in most of us and this is hooked to our perceptions directly. Persons of average sensitivity find the torture and maiming of small children repulsive; few fail to respond when directly exposed to piercing screams of pain or debilitating hunger.

Mediation appears to interfere with this hookup or to counteract its natural effects. We deny that we are autonomous agents in causing misery, we maintain that there is nothing we can do to alleviate it or, in coldest blood, we give some mad ideological reason why things ought to be this way or at least why they are best left alone. Most remarkable of all, we do not believe our eyes; we simply refuse to allow our senses to bring natural decency into play.

The social policy of requiring agents at the center to appropriate their distant acts and those at the periphery to examine the acts commanded to see if they might not be below human dignity to perform, would do more to alleviate human suffering than any other new law we could make. Both parts of such a policy would aim at causing individuals to transcend their narrow roles. The initiator of a mediated chain would be compelled to view himself as the cause of far-flung effects. He would have to familiarize himself with consequences and ways of life, knowledge of which is not required by his narrow role. The ultimate executor at the other end of the chain would be unavoidably thrown back into himself to consult his moral sense. He would have to learn to let himself feel and to force himself to reflect prior to taking irreversible action. At both ends of the chain individuals would find it necessary to act and to think as persons and not merely as temporary occupants of a formal office.

Admittedly, no society can continue to operate if every individual weighs each of his acts and may reject any of them at the bidding of his conscience. We owe an obligation to the institutions whose members we are, even if only because in playing a role in them we affect the lives of individuals. We also have a responsibility to those persons whom our private actions affect. In cases where the two obligations conflict, the situation is always difficult and unclear. When the attorney general was directed by President Nixon to fire Special Prosecutor Cox, his obligations were clearly in conflict. The difficulty of the situation is well shown by the fact that we celebrated the deep moral sense of the two attorneys general who, in quick succession, refused to carry out the order, while we could see adequate justification for the third to have obeyed his boss. What is required in such situations is not any given decision by those involved, but only a conscientious decision. And that cannot be one that flows solely from the internal dynamics of one's role. The person's relation to his role must always be taken into account; we must ever be mindful that it is not the role that acts or makes us act. On the contrary, we act and may choose to do so on the basis of what the role demands.

The objection that the introduction of personal decision into the chain of command destroys it is as fatuous as the famous objection to legalizing homosexuality that if it were allowed, the human race would very soon expire. It is absurd to suppose that what keeps us from passionately embracing others of our sex is the illegality of it all. If starvation were against the law and the ban were lifted, it is unlikely that large numbers would rush to deny themselves the pleasure of good meals. Legal or illegal, most people simply do not have much interest in being homosexuals.

Similarly, the vast bulk of mediated acts do not require agonizing personal decisions. With a little education and some practice people should be able to recognize cases which call for a hard decision. At any rate, they can be relied on not to think too much. Our natural tendencies and our desire for the easy and clearcut should save us from useless moral bafflement. The important thing is to keep the primacy of the person always in mind and to be ever alert to the situation in which we must act not like employees or soldiers or professionals, but like human beings.

Hegel uncovered a profound truth when he wrote of the importance of the sovereign in the state. It is not, of course, that monarchy is a particularly good form of government. The role of the head of state is not to make the laws or to govern. He serves as a personal symbol of the impersonal mechanisms of the nation. Rule by committee, Hegel well understood, is deeply disquieting to the populace. Citizens can identify with the abstract organism that is the state only to a certain point. Beyond that, they are in search of something they can understand and feel with; something that is simple, subjective, personal. Mediation has created patterns of interaction too complex to be readily grasped by most of us. The state is not only faceless, it is also radically beyond the scale of our senses and imagination. The desire to personify it is a natural unconscious attempt on our part to counteract mediation and to escape the psychic distance it creates.

The urge to escape the effects of mediation by personifying its creations is present now no less than it was in Hegel's day. We find it satisfying to think of corporations as bearing the stamp of the men who, we want to believe, created them. The president of the nation is conceived as somehow symbolizing its strength, resolve and moral character. Pictures of him hang in all government offices not because he is the favorite sight of civil servants or because of the unusual attractiveness of his countenance. He is there as the visible symbol of an enormously complex and in many respects unintelligible single community.

Even though the Stalinist cult of personality has been officially banned in socialist countries, the desire to transcend mediation by personifying important institutions and social policies persists. Likenesses of Lenin and of assorted other dignitaries glare at one in every public place. And one finds the solemn faces of Marx and Engels at each parade as mute symbols of the unity of all Communist parties. A related phenomenon can be observed in transcendent religions, where adoration is sometimes directed away from an abstract and invisible deity to his immediate representative in our midst. The leaders of cults know how to take advantage of this for personal profit as much as for the good of their believers. Even in Christianity one can legitimately wonder how much religious devotion stops at the person of the mediating evangelist and how many of his followers are truly carried through him to that invisible Person whom the Prayer Book calls our "only Mediator and Advocate."

The number of people in the world, or even in our country, and the variety of their interactions are beyond effective human conception. We can handle the variety in generalities and we can handle the numbers by means of statistics. These will give us ideas, but the ideas remain bare: they are not human in their scope and they are not effective in motivating persons. The larger the institutions which are sustained by mediation, the less human they appear and the less controllable they in fact become. In addition to the slippage that is inevitable in any single extended chain, we also face the drift that is due to the unplanned and unpredictable interaction of divergent chains.

Before long, it becomes evident that in a crowded world some of our important purposes can be achieved only by the introduction of centralized control. Ways are found by which the initiators of mediated chains can increase the likelihood that their desires are carried out by those on the periphery. And to minimize the harm that comes from the uncontrolled interaction of institutions in a social jungle, centralized government begins to flex its muscles. The growth of big government is due not to a conspiracy of self-important men bent on achieving control over our lives. On the contrary, it grows naturally and without design. Its role is partly to provide social services without which a large society could not operate and partly to prune the undesirable excesses of unlimited competition.

Government grows, as any successful social institution does, by feeding on itself. Its negative function of imposing limits on interaction is gradually converted into the positive role of setting social goals and providing centralized direction for the community. The development of a huge bureaucracy is, in this way, the natural and perhaps inevitable outcome of the need to control large institutionalized chains of mediation. The remarkable result is that the attempt at controlling mediated chains quickly generates the most uncontrolled, largest, and for this reason most dehumanized, structure of mediation.

6 Government Mediation

It is easy to see how another acts on my behalf when he does so because I ask him to or because he and I made a contract. One can then trace the causality of the action even though the ultimate agent may be far removed from my initial request. I may ask a friend to bid one of his foreign students to write his family in Biafra to send me stamps. Even when the request is open-ended or relatively indeterminate, such as when I ask a well-connected colleague to find someone to make me a loan, I know precisely who initiated the chain and I understand (and hope) that those in it are at work for me.

The way in which institutions perform actions on my behalf is much more difficult to see. For here things can come about not only because of a conscious request. In some cases no individual request is necessary or possible. and even where there is a contract between me and the institution, much of what it does to meet its part of the bargain is likely to be beyond my ken. What the electric company does in order to provide the power needed for lights and heating is altogether beyond the grasp of most of its customers. They do not know what the money they pay is used for; the fact that paying an electric bell might make them a party to strip mining and air pollution would not normally come to their attention.

The main obstacle to seeing an institution as acting on our behalf is that we cannot readily view ourselves as initiating its actions. It appears simply to be there as a center of ongoing activity. It exists ready to provide services before I contract with it and continues to exist even if I terminate my agreement. Its activity appears to be continuous and independent of whatever I might do. When I sign up for electric service the clerk does not flash the nearest coal-fired plant to jack up output now that Lachs is on board. The utility ties me into the existing power grid; I am inevitably led to feel that the only action my contract initiates is in the bookkeeping department.

Since I cannot see in the institution actions started specifically for me, I find it difficult to view myself as in any way responsible for what it does. But in fact the contract I sign with it makes me its partner. For a time, in limited but important ways, our fates are tied together. Its fortunes affect my life and mine may well influence our relationship. Although I cannot control what my partner does, I encourage it with regular contributions. Payment for services received is not a neutral or isolated act. Paying for the product earns me a share of the responsibility incurred in producing it. It may not appear this way, but the moment I pay for services they are performed *for me*, and I become an heir to their effects. One cannot buy the benefit of acts without inheriting their costs.

Benefits and costs, then, come in a single package: in buying the one we automatically obtain the other, as well. This is true in securing necessary goods no less than in contracting for services. Those who oppose the slaughter of animals sometimes maintain that they would never have a creature killed for them. Yet they buy meat and furs with the explanation that these are from animals already dead. Once the creature is dead, it must not be allowed to go unused; in buying its remains they honor it by not allowing it to have died in vain. For some inexplicable reason it never occurs to these fervent moralists that by buying the meat they become partners in the ongoing slaughter. They would give no verbal encouragement to the operator of the slaughterhouse. Yet could verbal comfort ever match the praise hard cash confers on the efforts of a businessman?

If it is difficult to view ourselves as active with respect to diverse social institutions which mediate our acts, it is doubly so in our relationship to the mechanisms of the state. For it takes a voluntary act on our part to initiate a relation with any existing social structure. Contracts must be entered, accounts opened, clubs joined. When things do not work out, the connection can be severed. At the least, one can go back to the time of initial agreement and rehearse the reasons for the union.

There is nothing like this in our relation to government. Our membership in a state is involuntary and automatic. It follows upon birth, and birth is not something we do but something that, as some would say, befalls us. We grow up belonging to a state, yet for the most part we are only half-conscious of this union. The benefits we derive from it appear natural; the relation rises to full consciousness only when we come up against the vexing limits of the law. The state provides citizens with ritualistic times and occasions designed to remind them of the benefits and burdens of their station. National feasts, election days and the annual deadline for filing tax returns call attention again and again to the gigantic organization in whose bowels we starve or thrive.

Yet this structure appears so distant from us, its elements are so well hidden because they are all-pervasive, that few of us have a clear idea how the state acts and in what ways our lives are in its hands. To some persons highways and sewer services appear no less natural than trees. They understand little of the effort that goes into converting nature to human use. Civilization is a work of art; cities and roads and aqueducts are built and maintained in the teeth of continued natural decay. Someone must bear the cost of this. In a just society, everyone does.

The problem is that without initial contract with the state, and so long as our continued support of it takes the form of routine acts, we have little to counteract the effects of its mediation. The state mediates a large number of our acts, some of them vital for continued survival. Yet the distance between us and its actions on our behalf is so vast that it transcends bafflement in the direction of utter ignorance. Social services have to be provided and laws must be passed to regulate the interaction of the populace. There must be some arrangement for the common defense. The rules established must be effectively enforced. All of this requires layered clusters of agencies within the government. A vast and intricate web of governmental organs develops to accomplish needed tasks. In the Middle Ages some philosophers postulated a separate potentiality for every act. Sometimes it appears that central bureaucracy grows in just such a way, generating a special agency for every special task.

We have in government a set of momentously complex chains of intermediaries. The complexity is perhaps greater that it need be; government, if it were designed, might be sparse yet elegantly effective. But, like all institutions of mediation, it is a natural growth and therefore luxuriant, a little haphazard and always laden with warts. And because one of the fundamental roles of government is to safeguard the social welfare, it shows endless reluctance to create unemployment by abolishing agencies once their task is done. The result is a bureaucracy whose lines of mediation are so interwoven that even those within may not know who else in government is doing something that contravenes or duplicates their efforts. The mechanism that is to provide central direction for society itself develops the need for a mechanism of central direction.

The reason for the inefficiency is only partly haphazard growth and the unwillingness to allow attrition. Sheer size makes some things unmanageable; in human institutions this occurs because of the slippage in mediated chains. In government the matter is aggravated by the very large number of intermediaries in each chain, as well as by the jumble of ill-organized, overlapping and rival chains. One result is that few know much and no one knows enough. Persons in the middle of chains find themselves as pure intermediaries, handing on orders, answering memos, writing reports. Their total official existence is exhausted in paperwork; they have no knowledge of how the decisions they hand on were made nor of the impact their execution will have. Decision makers have little understanding of how their policies are put into effect and what their rules look and feel like in reality. The eyes have high ideals but they forget the stubborn limitations of the hands. Finally, the little people carrying out policies at the far end of the chain feel as though they were tools of a colossal machine. Their jobs require them to carry out orders they did not help to make and whose effects they, better than anyone up the line, can see to be disastrous. The father in the National Guard may be mobilized and ordered with guns to the campus of his child.

The citizen who is most vitally affected by government edicts is normally least able to understand their rationale. He, and perhaps he alone, knows where the policies work hardship, where there may be need for a change in the rules or at least for an exception to them. Yet the civil servants with whom he deals feel that their hands are tied. They act out their roles and are reluctant to make a decision which transcends routine, even if they have the authority. In the interaction of citizen and government, therefore, we find once again the classic signs of large-scale mediation: roles overshadow humanity, the interacting agents feel helpless and victimized, the patterns of action become rigid and slip from control. The citizen then begins to perceive government as distant, uninformed and uncaring. In a dictatorship unvented anger focuses on a man; it is satisfying to think that his wickedness is the cause of our pain. In a democratic society, even this pleasure of a personified focus for our hate is denied us. Instead, we speak of "Washington"—a faceless city—as the source of misery.

Calling the imagined source of trouble "Washington" or "City Hall" reveals a great deal of our state of mind. We think of the center as impersonal. It is not controlled by individuals; in the end, perhaps, no one is responsible for where we are and no one can make a difference for the future. There is no one to confront, none that could listen to entreaties or respond to threats. The machine runs itself, out of the control of Congress, presidents. At the storm center of it all is an empty force, like the nothingness which in the middle of an onion surrounds itself with layered, pungent growths. This psychic distance from the faceless center is framed in impotence. It is tinged with the bitterness that comes of knowing that although we are not in command of the machine, we must pay for its operation.

It is the absence of an initial voluntary act in joining a nation that makes the fiction of the social contract attractive. For in that contract we once made—or continually make—a free commitment to social life with all its burdens and its benefits. It is the voluntariness of the contract that matters; a free commitment is open to review and confers on us the right to terminate. Rousseau and others add to this notion the noble thought that society is but an extension of the self. Rightly conceived, this makes government the organ of our self-determination. Government edicts are not, then, alien forces that constrain. On the contrary, they are rules designed to form and guide our social self. They are expressions of our will; we must embrace them as our own. Our representatives are temporarily empowered to speak on our behalf. As such, they make *our* decisions. And government officials are but agents in carrying out our will; they ought to be what, today only by hyperbole, we call them—civil *servants.*

Mediation is at the very heart of this conception of the nature and legitimacy of government. Its striking feature is the recognition that governmental mediation generates problems of psychic distance which we must take special steps to combat. In representative democracy, government is thought to be justified only through the consent of the governed. An initial act of authorizing must, therefore, undergird the authority of officials. What right has any government agent to tell me what to do? If he is not to be a self-appointed busybody whose instructions should evoke only annoyance or mirth, he must have a valid claim to our allegiance.

Hobbes recognized this and attempted to derive the valid claim by an analysis of how government acquires the right to command. The person who has the initial right or freedom to perform a given action he calls its "author"; the individual who actually performs it is said to be the "actor." Actor and author may, of course, be one and the same person in a given case. But circumstances may arise in which the author cannot or prefers not to act. He may then convey his right to perform the act or to make the decision to another. When the right is properly conveyed, the actor is said to be "authorized"; he has been given the right to act on behalf of someone else. This is essentially what we do when we elect representatives and senators. We ask them to act for us; in doing so, we assign to them our right to make certain decisions.

Although they are authorized mediators of our actions, there are limits to what elected representatives may do. The authority they acquire is conditional, limited and revocable. It is conditional, or else public officials would not have to take an oath of office. Occupancy of a post is dependent not only on election or appointment, but also on the continuing fulfillment of the duties specified in the oath. It is limited, or else tenure of public office would be indefinite and its power uncontrolled. In fact, authority is conferred for a specific length of time to do a more or less specific set of things, and under no circumstances for doing *whatever* seems advisable *at any time*. And it is revocable, or else once in authority, public officials would be free from accountability. But if they are found guilty of certain sorts of negligence or wrongdoing, they may be impeached and removed from office before their term expires.

The growth of psychic distance between the representative and his constituency is inevitable. He acts on behalf of thousands at a considerable physical and mental remove. We send him or her to Washington, where he is exposed to experiences, pressures and arguments the nature and very existence of which are hidden from us. He conducts his own study of problems, listens to others with perspectives divergent from his and learns the fine art of compromise. Although not everything is a fit subject for legislation, we send him with the right to cast his ballot on any and every bill introduced. This includes subjects that are not only far from our concerns but actually outstrip our understanding and competence. They may also outstrip his.

The representative learns things we have neither the time nor the opportunity to learn. Ideally, he grows in understanding without losing his concern for what the folks back home might want to see him do. But, inevitably, as he grows he leaves the provincial orbit of our minds. He becomes cosmopolitan perhaps, or a little too sophisticated. At any rate, the reasons he sees for his actions rarely reach us, and when they do we may not share his view of their power. The man the people elected as the man of the people thus becomes baffling to them. At home he still seems like the person he used to be: he walks on Main Street with his sleeves rolled up, shakes hands and wants to know about the corn. But his official actions seem not to fit in; how could a man so homespun say the things he says on foreign policy?

In light of the real position of the legislator, the problem of whether he merely reflects the will of his constituency or makes his own decisions is contrived. He may not be in a position to express the will of his people, even if he knows just what it is. Of course, for the most part he does not and perhaps he cannot know. For he is no less distant from their state of mind than they are from his. He may conduct polls and spend every weekend on home turf in a trailer seeing the people who put him in his job. Yet the national context in which his votes are cast, his daily life in a distant capital are not just passing clouds in his changeless sky. They make him who he is by shaping his thoughts and feelings.

His decisions, though taken on our behalf, are therefore his, not ours. He may know what we think or at least what some small number of us hold, but he evaluates these thoughts, places them in perspective as but one factor, and then decides. It is impossible for him to be merely a mouthpiece for others. The question with which he must struggle is not whether his votes mirror the ideas of his constituents; if that is all he tried to do, disagreement among the folks back home would have him vote both yea and nay. His genuine concern must be to find a way in which his decisions can be responsive to the deeper, hidden wisdom of his people. He must try to subserve and express the interests, the largely unconscious impulses and commitments of those whose will he bears.

This is a tall order for ordinary mortals. And it is made more difficult by the fact that a leader must not be more than a step or two ahead of the people he represents. If he knows his people's deepest will, he may know too much. He must bring out what may perhaps be unconscious in them but is ready to be raised to light; if he goes too far too fast, he soon finds himself alone. His constituents must be able to appropriate his actions as their own; without that, he will appear as a scheming politician or idealistic fool.

Here the representative in a large democracy is up against overwhelming odds. He needs not only instinctive wisdom in knowing his people and the tact and patience not to do too much. He must also have the time, talent and commitment to educate. He must bring his people along so that they get to know themselves better and learn to see their narrow wants in the broader perspective of an uncertain future and a crowded nation. And even if he succeeds to some extent in this difficult undertaking, he has managed to reduce the psychic distance only between his people and *his* acts. But he is only one of many delegates; his votes are but one tactor in making policy. Even if he fights for what we want, the opposite of what he votes for may become the law. His constituents may well find themselves in harmony with his thoughts and yet at a great distance from the government. For they may discover that their lives are controlled not by the votes of their homely deputy, but by the distant desires of alien countrymen.

For this reason, the larger the nation, the greater is the distance between citizen and government. The more mediated chains converge in the capital, the less those of us on the periphery of the chains can see the actions of the central body as our own. The diversity of interests and perspectives creates compromises which may represent no one's will to an adequate extent. We thus face a growing distance not only from our own representatives, but also from our countrymen far away. We may feel that we are asked to share burdens without receiving benefits, we may resent the influence of the people of other regions on laws that govern our lives, we may even experience their effect on government as oppressive. The individual may then come to feel that self-determination has completely slipped from his grasp. For even if he can identify with his authorized representative, he soon finds himself confronted with the unpalatable fact that control over his life is not in the hands of this man. Laws are ultimately made by the delegates of everybody else; our own senator or representative controls neither the framing of the laws nor their execution.

Any citizen who thinks of laws and social policies as the medium of his self-determination must, therefore, think of the entire nation, of all his fellow citizens, as constituting his extended self. And there is, perhaps, a sense in which a nation is a unitary whole: the close causal interconnection through production, transportation, distribution and communication of all regions clearly points to this. But even if the continued successful operation of the entire country is a condition of my life and prosperity, I may not be in a position to grasp my dependence on the larger social self. For the bonds that tie me to my countrymen and neighbors are subtle and complex chains of mediation. They twist from me as relative center like roads winding in every direction. If followed, they would take me everywhere; everyone could then perhaps be seen as my brother or neighbor. But I cannot follow all roads and my horizon reflects the limits of a busy, minor mind. I cannot imagine what people are like in far corners of my land, and even if I can imagine it, I cannot sympathize. The Kansas farmer is an abstract thought, terror in San Francisco is but news, the Southern redneck is a stereotype. The unintelligible interests of unknown people shape our lives. Control over the fortunes of the self by the social whole may well be self-determination, but it feels like the dominion of an alien force.

The distancing of citizens from their government does not end with what is experienced as alien control over the creation of laws. The laws are administered by an unwieldy bureaucracy. The chains there stretch to every hamlet from the capital. To combat slippage, the operational procedures within the chains are rigidly defined. To avoid injustice, each link in the chain is permitted some leeway or official discretion. Yet in long chains where control slips and structuring intentions are subverted, each safeguard tends to cause effects which contravene the purpose for which it was designed. Rigidity in following directives then becomes a source of blind inhumanity and discretion in applying the rules breeds inequality and malicious caprice.

Even the directives produced tend to be distant and faulty. This, again, is due to extensive mediation. Upper level civil servants have even less contact with the daily lives of grassroot citizens than elected representatives. They do not need to stand for reelection and can in any case view themselves as neutral administrators of the will of others. The result is that their regulations remain abstract and impractical. Since the experience of those most directly affected is unsought or disregarded, rules designed to benefit people frequently end up as irrelevant to their condition or divorced from their needs.

The demand for efficiency causes bureaucrats to restrict their chain of mediation to their superiors and subordinates. In fact, however, this tends to keep the executive chain ineffective. By a strange paradox, if the chain were extended to include individuals whom the rules affect, it could become more effective and generate less resentment and distress. Continued consultation with people who are the butt of legislative action reduces psychic distance. The administration of laws becomes easier, acceptance of regulations more spontaneous. But bureaucratic organizations abhor public presence in their operations no less than nature was supposed to shun a vacuum. I once heard a high official earnestly explain that one can consult too much. He, at any rate, was in no danger of this, having done none in years. He professed amazement at the reluctance of people to accept rules written by experts aimed at public good. He was so close to the hub of executive chains, his mind was so infected with the provinciality of the center that he found the equal legitimacy of a divergent perspective unthinkable. To him those to be governed had but partial thoughts; their perceptions were subjective and sharply limited.

Such drive for efficiency and expertise naturally points to a paternalistic totalitarian regime. The aim of totalitarianism is not to stamp out the individual. Frequently it is oppressive not by design but only as things turn out or in our experience of it. The ideal of the totalitarian is social integration on the basis of central plans. His aim is social welfare, his instrument the ubiquitous expert, his product an organic state that meets human needs. To achieve these, only vagrant personal desires and public participation in decisions need be sacrificed. And this is no great loss in the eyes of a totalitarian. For to him private wants have little social import and public presence in the decision-making process does nothing to improve the judgment of the experts.

Since the price of consensus is too high for the friend of totality, he attempts to create synthetic agreement through propaganda. And where indoctrination fails, he resorts to the judicious use of power to enforce compliance. In the search for efficiency in our pursuit of goals, police power will always seem more effective, simpler and less costly than the immense effort required to educate and through ideas or incentives to motivate a reluctant populace. Centralized police action is, therefore, not a primary aim of totalitarian regimes; it is the price they pay for rapid progress toward some distant goal.

The presence of such an external goal, usually involving order and organized happiness, is a fundamental mark distinguishing a society of mediated chains that has reached the totalitarian stage from one we would conventionally call democratic. The goal of a democracy is not some definite future condition of the state. Its primary ideal is to get wherever it may go as a result of free social agreement. The aim thus is to perfect a process of decision-making and through that to enable each individual to feel his unity with the social whole. Giving each person a say and a felt personal stake in what is done by all is a staggeringly inefficient way of achieving anything. But this matters little if there is no major communal objective beyond the perfection of a process and the products that offers. The attainment of such excellence requires continual education, the creation of mechanisms for informing the average citizen and for involving him in the governmental process. A natural by-product of such large-scale education is growth in the ability of individuals to make intelligent decisions for themselves.

The moment we see this we recognize that the essence of democratic government is, as Mill correctly remarked, the moral education of the populace. This is a training in freedom for the purpose of making us free, and the nurture of our intellects so that our freedom may be enlightened and our practice keen-eyed. All social decisions in a democracy, therefore, take back seat to the activity by which we arrive at them. For the ultimate social commitment is to the development of human freedom and character, and perhaps only as a condition of that development of character, to welfare.

This may sound idealistic, and it must if it is to be accurate. For I am describing the frequently unrecognized and rarely uttered ideal of democratic rule. What makes it merely an ideal is the omnipresence of long mediated chains in industrial society. Mediated chains institutionalize the division of tasks and invite the rule of the expert. They naturally distance the locus of decision-making from most of us. The chain long enough and numerous enough to operate a country such as ours make genuine public involvement in decisions taken on behalf of the public prohibitively expensive. To educate the nation on each step it must take, to move it to conscious involvement in each social design and law and policy, requires a momentous effort. For a busy bureaucrat this at once implies that the cost is too high, for it leaves little energy for the conduct of the actual business of the central government.

Is this implication just? The bureaucrat's perception of the undesirably high cost of education in public affairs is shaped by his role, which sets him at a great psychic distance from his charges. This distance removes their self-improvement as a real goal. Its place is taken by efficiency, a native aim of each bureaucracy. And rules backed by force appear more efficient than persuasion, which is costly and yields uncertain results. The most democratic-minded civil servant finds himself, therefore, in the midst of chains naturally propelled toward totalitarianism. He learns to think that his value is measured in objective achievements, that time spent in educating those he governs is unfortunately wasted.

If civil servants could redirect their thinking and consider no achievement worthwhile unless it is the result of joint action, they would find the burden of governing considerably lightened. They might not have much energy left after the education and motivation of the people. But there would be little energy needed for anything else. For a willing and intelligent population is easy to govern; once the motive is internalized, there is little need for external controls. As things are, universal participation in social decision-making is not an alluring ideal. Freedom and self-determination are not visible goods; no one can point to the improved character of a people and take pride in it as we do in good highways or an army.

For this reason, the public decision-making process is rarely viewed as anything but a means to public ends, a strategy used by government to gain social acceptance of its goals. To bring democracy to full bloom, we need to redirect our thinking. We must learn to view public decision-making as an activity and not as a process whose justification resides in the product it creates. As an activity, public self-determination becomes its own end. It does not thereby cease to have results: decisions are reached and implemented, policies are designed and put into effect. But, important as these effects are, they become secondary to the exercise of freedom that brought them into being and endowed them with legitimacy.

The chains of mediation that run from the bureaucratic center to the home and life of every citizen naturally create a psychic distance between the government and the people. As the chains grow, so does the distance, until each act of the central government creates its own credibility gap. The people, naturally given to reading purposes even into mechanical slippage, begin to talk of a conspiracy of politicians and bureaucrats. In fact, there is of course no such conspiracy. There may even be a great deal of good will all around. But ignorance of each others' motives and perceptions renders the actions of each side incomprehensible to the other. Ignorance breeds suspicion and suspicion feeds on itself. Soon the social fabric is rent and what holds us together is no longer desire and felt unity, but force or fear or the lack of an alternative.

It need not be this way. Substantial public participation in governmental decision-making could make for domestic peace and social unity. The strategies for achieving such large-scale citizen involvement must be diverse and aggressive; they are likely to be costly in effort and in renounced government prerogatives. The doors and the lives of politicians, the files and the procedures of civil servants would have to be thrown open. The blessed anonymity of government decision-makers would have to be surrendered, and with this surrender would go increased accountability. Busy deputies in responsible positions would have to put up with some meddling; they might also find that they have to spend what appears to them endless hours explaining their positions. Mere openness and broad but cursory consultation will, of course, not do the job. The point is to get politicians and civil servants to view themselves as educators of the people. And this education cannot be one-sided. It has to be a partnership of the teachers and the taught in which each takes turn to educate the other.

The probability of anything like this actually taking place approaches zero or has already reached it. Nonetheless, it is important to spell out the ideal so that citizen groups and well-meaning legislators working for better government may consciously move in its direction. It is clear that at least one strategy frequently proposed will not work. Confronted with overlapping layers of government that reach from the county courthouse to the White House, nineteenth-century liberals (now called conservatives) usually propose to minimize regulation and reduce centralized control to the lowest practical level. According to this view, whatever can be reasonably left to the private decision of individuals or the operation of the marketplace should be free of government restraints. Local government should be given the responsibility of administering regulations to the limit of its ability; state government should step in only when municipal authorities fail. And the federal government should be allowed a say only in those matters which cannot be handled by the individual states.

This a worthy ideal, even though circumstances have made it outmoded. What makes it worthy is not only the insistence on individual freedom it involves, but also its tacit recognition that the least-mediated government, and hence the government that is at the least psychic distance from its people, is the best.

But the ideal is outmoded for two reasons. The first is that municipal government is as afflicted with problems of psychic distance today as is the most unwieldy federal agency. This might seem surprising in view of the relatively small size of the mediated chains involved in running a city or a county. But, in fact, the chains are longer than they seem. They involve not only elected members of government and municipal employees, but also important citizens and special interest groups. The latter frequently have a disproportionately strong influence on regulations adopted and the manner of their implementation. And it is important to remember that psychic distance is a function not only of the length of mediated chains, but also of the access peripheral members have to the center and of the differences between the interests and experiences of the members. The more directly special interest groups such as builders and land developers influence municipal government, the less opportunity others have of being heard. And the less weight they carry, especially with townsfolk and their neighbors, the more angry and frustrated ordinary citizens become.

The second reason why the ideal of maximum local government is outmoded relates to the nearly organic interconnection of all the parts of our country. Mediated chains are omnipresent and they do not stop at the county line. All of us are tied to one another by invisible chains of necessary interaction. One cannot control only one part of the chain. And it is grossly destructive of the social fabric to impose different rules and standards on each different part. The totality is present everywhere; it exerts its influence on each part of each chain. Less than centralized regulation remains, for this reason, rhapsodic and ineffectual. The complex interconnections in a populous mediated world require uniform rules and predictable enforcement.

Municipal and state government simply do not have the scope to cope with the corporation and the labor union. Big government is not an incidental growth or the product of conspiracy. A rich country with a large population invites broad commerce and big business. Big government is required to create safe conditions for big business, and also to control it. The desire for local autonomy is an idle dream. If it could be achieved—as it clearly cannot—newly uncontrolled labor and business would quickly make it a nightmare. Powerful central govenment has become a condition of our civilization: since our economy and our public services depend on it, we could simply not live or live well without it.

It sometimes appears that we cannot live with it, either. But this is not a fault of all government, only of government that takes no steps to mitigate mediation, that is paternalistic and operates at a remove. Big government must be accepted as a necessary force. But it must be turned into a medium of self-determination, into an instrument of freedom. not oppression.

7 Mediation Internalized

We have no adequate account of what goes on in the minds of our neighbors. Those who have devoted attention to the flow of consciousness have been thoughtful, self-conscious people describing what they found in their most thoughtful, self-conscious moments. Was the busy flux of feelings and ideas William James so eloquently portrayed in his famous account of the stream of consciousness really present to him at each waking moment? And even if it was present to him, is that anything more than a tribute to his active mind?

What are the thoughts of people in their sullen, quiet moments? If we could chart the ebb and flow of images and feelings that inhabit the mind of the commuter or the listener at the afterdinner speech, what would we get? We would find few ideas; long silences of sentience surround conventional sights. A lukewarm feeling might flower now and then, half-formed desires might flutter for a moment like birds nestling for the night. If some omniscient psychologist could observe this consciousness for traces of the self, he would find nothing or next to nothing to report. Our consciousness is thin and intermittent. The few sentiments we feel, the images that haunt us, relate to crises of some minor, personal sort or else result from the conventions of social life.

Little of the self is revealed in routine inner life, and what is revealed is a routine, social self. Physical objects and people around us mediate what goes on inside: they determine the form, the content and the occasion of our ideas. We serve only as the bearers of our thoughts. The impact of our common language is so great because this is the medium that shapes our judgments. Its structure sets sharp limits to what is thinkable. Agreement within society is not a matter of persuasion. Shared ideas and perspectives, due to no small extent to the shared heritage of language and culture, underlie the possibility of persuasion. The fundamental reality is common experience, uniform feelings, convergent perceptions.

We all know that the individual is largely a social creation. The young child is not a fully formed little savage who has to be socialized. The process of socialization is a creative one; it is the process of creating individuals. In the course of it society, acting through the agents that surround us, endows us with far more than social skills and a repertoire of behaviors. The habits, tendencies and attitudes that shape much of our later life are instilled in us at this stage. We are taught not only what to do but also how to feel about it. And, perhaps most important of all, we acquire a conceptual framework which then permanently shapes our perceptions and our thoughts. Specific beliefs and ideas are changeable and relatively insignificant if set over against these fundamental concepts and cognitive attitudes.

These facts may not always be as clearly before us as they should, but they are incontestable facts, nevertheless. To view them from the perspective of mediation is useful largely because of the unified context it provides and the otherwise hidden trends it reveals. First of all, the recognition that the self would not even exist if it were not for the mediating activity of our fellows, is a useful antidote to excessive individualism. But the full force of an analysis of the inner life and of outward self-expression from the standpoint of mediation cannot be felt until we move beyond the initial level of social person-making.

If the growing person remained an inert amalgam of external influences, there could be no significant conflict between the individual and society. The interests of the social whole could then never conflict with the interest of the single person, for having no unity of person or perspective, he would have no identifiable interests at all. But the personality is no less organic than the human body. All of the human body is made of external materials: it is brought into being out of materials that antedate it and are, therefore, initially not its own. And it can sustain itself in existence only by the continued assimilation of external stuff. Yet, by an everyday miracle, the body is not a heap of hamburgers and gravy, of chickens and chocolate cake. All of these are turned into one's substance; the body absorbs them, imposing its own form on divergent contents. Through it all, it retains its unity as a center of action, a focal point of differentiated energy.

The personality parallels the body in having an organic unity of its own. Though created by others out of materials initially alien to it, it soon appropriates these materials and organizes itself into a unit which stands as a swirling center of energy against the world. It is possible that personalities are less rigid than bodies; they might in happy circumstances grow a little more or else undergo metamorphosis and emerge as butterflies after an ugly start. But they are more or less successfully executed organic structures, patterns or melodies, nevertheless. Health and happiness are at least partly a function of how tightly or, at any rate, how coherently the unity holds.

The important thing to keep in mind is that personality, like the body, is an active unity, a unity within a constant flux. The center can be sustained only by the energetic absorption of new materials, by the readiness to appropriate what is brought to us by fortune and appetite. For this reason, if for no other, the self is perpetually engaged in the activity of creating itself. There is nothing mysterious about this. Saying it does not credit the human self with divine or superhuman powers. It is just that after the initial person-making acts of society, the person created takes over, to a considerable extent, the unavoidable task of continued self-creation. The way its past has been taken into its substance, the meanings it attaches to present stimuli, its wayward projects for a structured future all conspire to render the self the being that it is. They propel it to reproduce itself or else to change; in either case, every moment of experience is a renewed, if minor, challenge requiring response.

Those who stress the unfreedom of the self focus unduly on its constituents. They see that all its materials derive from past its borders, and therefore suppose that whatever it does is done or shaped by what makes it up and hence by an external force. What they fail to see is that the past resides in our personalities not in the way in which dead logs lie in the yard or indifferent chairs may be stacked four high in warehouses. The past is appropriated: it is made a part of who we are. If we act under its influence, it is nevertheless *we* who act. Since I am, among other things, my past, if it does anything, so do I. Or, better, if it acts at all, it can act only through me.

Nothing I have said implies, of course, that we are free in some deep metaphysical sense or that our actions are inexplicable and uncaused. I want to stress only that thinking about the human personality from the vantage point of simple mechanism is not really enlightening. The self is much less like a rope or a river or a piece of oxidizing steel than like an organic body which is the source of unitary acts. Its actions, though determined, are in the end its own. Its life, though the result of a conspiracy of desires and accidents, is ultimately a function of what it did and does.

Mediation for the adult, then, acquires a role and significance different from what it has in initial person-making acts. For the personality that gradually emerges as a result of the socialization of a child has at least the rudiments of organic unity. By slow degrees it takes possession of the task of self-creation. It learns to think for itself and to make its own decisions. It learns to deliberate and to choose among its desires. It masters the difficult arts of self-motivation and steadfast pursuit.

At a certain stage the individual is ready to be independent and self-determining. This is but another way of saying that at least for the purposes of deciding what to think and when to feel and how to live he could dispense with the mediation of others. He has presumably learned his lessons: here he no longer needs his parents or his peers. He might still watch their faces with some interest, but no longer to take a measure of his actions by their smiles. His independence need not be aggressive. He can take others into account, even plan so his actions will cause them happiness. What matters is that they be performed by him for his own and special reasons and not at the initiative of another or under another's influence.

This ideal of self-determination might be difficult to achieve, but it is not intrinsically unworkable. Its immediate implication is that, although mediation is inescapable in the social sphere and may be necessary even for continued physical survival, there is at least one realm which could be substantially exempt from it. Each individual could be an independent person due to choice, as Robinson Crusoe was by necessity. Even though he had little control over the setting and ultimate circumstances of his life, he learned to pattern his passing days and shape his future to express his self. His personality acquired an autonomy, his feelings and perceptions gained a sureness that far exceeded anything he had had back home. Of course, he could have had something resembling that internal independence even if he had never left his native York. Perhaps it would have been more difficult to gain it there; in any case, it would have required continued struggle to keep it intact. Society would have constantly forced, threatened or tempted him to take the easy way out and let it determine what he thought and when. But he was of a breed of Englishmen—single-minded and strong-willed—who might take everyone into account, yet in the end permit none to make his decisions.

Such self-determination has some kinship with the Stoic ideal. The Stoics were right in their insistence that happiness is integrally connected with a strong and independent personality. The man who bobbed like cork on the waters of fortune could enjoy all the pleasure the gods might decide to shower on him. But he could not *be* happy, even though on occasion he might *feel* as though he were. For true happiness is a stable state in which one's feelings and one's actions reflect or express one's personality. There is little reason to go beyond this with the Stoics. The pretense of cold indifference to everything that happens is an ideal of disembodied reason, not of breathing men. It is important to be open to the world. But we must weigh its message in the private mind. Autonomy is not unique to the hermit; if anything, he makes his victory cheap by simply excluding the world. The ideal is to allow the world to enter and yet not to lose one's soul.

The quality of a personality and the happiness of a person are determined by the extent to which he succeeds in eliminating the mediation of others in his private world. Let others think and say and do what they will; let it all be grist for that inner mill which is the immediate source of all our thoughts and feelings. The more uncritically we adopt the beliefs and lifestyles of others, the more our inner life is hostage to mediated chains. And when I speak of inner life, I mean the life of a person, not a mind. Thoughts and feelings are not private episodes in an impenetrable soul; beliefs and commitments are never free-floating structures in a private sky. There is an element of real privacy in every life, but everything hidden has also a public face. Our values show themselves in what we do, our thoughts in what we say. Our feelings burst forth like ill-disguised whores, soliciting, mock-shy, uncouth. All our public life is an expression of who we are, and all our inner life a reflection of what we do. Public and private always interact: we shape our actions to conform to self and create a self by doing what we do.

The moment we look at how things stand with personal independence in our world, we see a picture of cripples and mooncalves. We tend to judge the health of the person by external standards. If his body is intact, if his actions seem relatively sane, we are prepared to think of him as healthy. Emotional well-being and the development of personality are invisible goods: since they disclose themselves only to the inquisitive mind, they remain unthought of and unknown to most of us. Imagine what people would look like if, by some strange inversion, their personalities were fully revealed to the naked eye. Dorian Gray could not bear the sight of a single face, his own, that showed the scars of emotional abuse. If our bodies were invisible and our moral persons manifest, we might well follow the lead of Oedipus and blind ourselves rather than see such sights.

The primacy of the visible body is very clear even in the laws we make. The criminal code is focused on preventing persons from doing harm to one another. Harm is typically limited to physical, visible or measurable maiming. If the laws are extensive and rigid enough, I may find myself in a position where I can hardly touch the body of another without the potential for felony. Yet, paradoxically, there is very little I cannot do to my fellows to cripple their soul. Teachers inflict the greatest indignities on their students every day. No one has ever tried to gauge the damage unthinking

99

parents do to their offspring. Advertisers foster the basest elements in our nature. What is presented for our enjoyment through the media inevitably creates false beliefs about how the world works and what we ought to do. All of these are legal, accepted, even respectable pursuits. Yet any one of them can do more damage than a beating or a dozen robberies.

The same lack of attention or lack of respect for inner health is shown by gevernment licensing procedures. There are elaborate rules for certifying the competence of physicians and nurses and pharmacists. Yet virtually anyone can be a teacher. And there are no requirements whatever for being a parent. Admittedly, incompetence in a physician might result in death. But the far more widespread incompetence of teachers and parents results in crippled adults, many of whom feel that they might as well be dead. There is more actual abuse in the rearing and education of children today than there is potential for abuse in all of medicine.

Some think that it is not in the interest of society to permit the development of independent persons. But they conceive society's interests too narrowly. On a broader view, if the development of a full personality is in the interest of individuals, it must in the end also be in the interest of society. For the social whole is nothing but the collection of individuals that compose it; what benefits them cannot be alien to the whole they constitute.

However this may be, it is clear that the mechanism involved in our widespread personal impoverishment is that of mediation. Perhaps a full personality can develop only in a mediated world: the lonely savage who ekes out a miserable existence is not likely to serve as an ideal of well-rounded fulfillment. But if mediation is a condition of personality development, it is also an impediment to it. For a heavily mediated industrial society does not require mature independence in its citizens, nor is such personal independence conducive to its smooth operation. It thrives, instead, by spearing the inner life of individuals and stringing it on a chain to manipulate. Social control is made easy in proportion to the uniformity of thought and feeling a society can achieve in its citizens.

The vast majority of us are cripples, then, if judged in terms of the potential for inner independence. Our beliefs are determined by the prevailing climate of opinion. Our thoughts, feelings and attitudes belong to others and only because of that to us; in having or undergoing them we do what others would have us do. Independent judgment is rare and difficult. There is comfort in agreement with the multitude or, if we think of ourselves as iconoclasts, then at least in mouthing the orthodoxies of the unorthodox. Everything bears against self-determination in what we believe. Too many matters are too technical or require skills we could never master. In science, in law, in government we are surrounded by experts who devote their lives to studying what we will never know. Physicians and nurses, ministers and psychiatrists jealously guard their secret competence. We could never be experts in all things, and since there are experts in every field, we think it best to defer to their authority.

The Middle Ages are usually thought of as a period of great reliance on authority. In fact, for the average man, ours is an age in which the weight of authority is far greater. The source of authority has changed; but concurrently with this, its scope has undergone a vast expansion. In the Middle Ages authority was concentrated; this very concentration in church and king left belief in a variety of spheres altogether optional. The decentralization of authority has given us authorities everywhere: each person wants to claim the prerogatives of knowledge in some minuscule sphere. No one has the time or energy to master everything; the result is a remarkable mixture of aggressive omniscience in a minute field with passive credulence everywhere else.

But it is not only a lack of time and competence that stops us from thinking for ourselves. And it is not just comfort or laziness that makes us agree with the herd. Frequently the very facts that would enable us to judge for ourselves are not available. Nowhere is this more evident than in public affairs. The standard response on the part of government officials to criticism leveled against their decisions is that those who object have no access to the facts. If only citizens had all the special information politicians and civil servants do, so the argument runs, they would understand the rationale of the decision and, presumably, agree. Yet why is the information unavailable to most of us? Admittedly, some of it is a matter of the untransmittable perspective of one's special slot in the chain of mediation. But most of it is clearly the result of an unreasonable desire for government secrecy.

Government secrecy is so widespread and, in spite of occasional leaks, so secure that we do not even know what things we know nothing about. There are special advantages to systematic stealth. If knowledge confers power, exclusive knowledge makes power private and secure. It also reduces accountability: if we do not know what an official knew at the time of his decision, it is hard to show that his actions were wrong. And, finally, the dependence of mediated chains is considerably enhanced if the knowledge of those in the chains is minimized. That way, after each narrow operation they have to come back for their instructions to be renewed. This adds to the sense of one's own importance. It also tends to stabilize the chains. In this way, mediated chains remain chains of command and the chance of independent action is reduced.

The news media make occasional raids on government secrecy. Yet they themselves fall short of providing the facts to back individual thought. It is not that they are engaged in a conspiracy to deny us access to what we should know. On the contrary, they are happy to provide every useless scrap of scandal and gossip. But the very essence of news gathering is selectivity and the selection always reflects the perspective and commitments of the reporter involved. The problem is nothing as simple as what reporters are warned against when they first go on the job—it is not a matter of carelessly editorializing on the front page. Selectivity operates on a much more subtle and much less easily controlled level. It shows itself not in what strikes the reporter's fancy but in what comes to his attention in the first place. Unless he is sensitized to certain possibilities, unless he has developed certain perspectives and concepts, some central facts may altogether escape him. The selectivity is already there in what he notes. This is evident if one compares reports of the same event in this country and in the Soviet Union. A similar though less striking difference can be seen between reporters in your home town: all one needs to do is to read the presumably factual accounts of the same tragedy in the morning and in the afternoon paper.

The selectivity which shows itself in what newsmen note

appears again in what they decide to stress. They write or video-tape or photograph for the public; their interest is naturally focused on what they think might attract public attention. The emphasis on the sensational is, therefore, natural. But no matter how natural it is, it tends to distort. For the unusual plucked out of its context invites misinterpretation. A quick closeup of a pool of blood followed by the grim face of an armed policeman conveys an image of brutality, even if the blood is a struck dog's and the officer looks grim because of the flu. The reporter's choice of words, the juxtaposition of facts, the entire structure of the story communicate meanings far beyond what the individual sentences express. The reporter actually creates the entire story in the reader's mind. Since what he writes is all we actually know of the matter, how he presents the facts naturally shapes our interpretation of them. This is the real power of the media. They gather the news the way bees collect pollen; what we get is the honey they spit out.

How can we begin to form our own opinions if the time, the skills and the facts are often wanting? In the face of such helplessness, Bertrand Russell and others recommend the ultimate in personal defense. We are to be sceptical of everything we hear, and doubt both the report and the reporter until verified. But this is a prescription only for making us feel a little better or smarter, not for practical life. We do not have the time to question nor the opportunity to check every fact. Yet we must continue to live and act as if we knew. Daily life cannot reflect universal doubt; we can suspend some judgments, but we cannot suspend our lives. If reason holds back assent, we have to act without belief. Our cautious minds then become isolated from daily concerns and can never escape self-wrought impotence. The motivation behind this scepticism is exceptionally fine: we should all refuse to be mislead. But applied in practice it soon becomes absurd. It stresses private judgment and the need to know to the point where action is cut loose from thought and we lose the chance to choose.

Our autonomy of choice is heavily infringed, as it is. We find ourselves in a situation which permits us little control over what to do. Governmental decisions, which for the most part escape our influence, set sharp limits to the range of our acts. Most of us work for others; this is but another way of saying that for the bulk of almost every day we surrender the right to do what we desire. Through their needs and rights and deeds, others make our decisions for us even in private life, in homes and churches and at the grocery store. Some of these decisions are made with our consent and many of them may well be to our benefit. But they are mediated decisions, nonetheless, choices we have not shaped that shape us. For if someone else frames my intention, the action I perform is primarily his, not mine. Our ability, itself not inconsiderable, to appropriate these decisions, to make the best of what others have us do, does not change the fact that we are often passive in giving direction to our lives.

Government has to assure compliance with its edicts. The simplest way is to impose laws and to enforce them with vigor. A more costly way, in growing disrepute, is to provide incentives: to weight our choices so that we feel inclined to opt for the desired actions. There are some, particularly Marxists engaged in social critique, who fail to see or to acknowledge that there is a real difference between these two ways of attaining order. They feel that both involve coercion or the use of government force. There is some truth to this, for the provision of punishments and rewards to influence our choice itself requires great discretionary power. Nevertheless, there is a crucial difference between the two ways of operation. The first involves the employment of naked force which creates fear and submission without any choice. The second leaves it up to the individual to choose for himself and then bear the follow-up. It is important that the choice be genuine: if there are no real alternatives or if one of the alternatives is too heavily weighted, we may have a case of force masquerading as popular choice. Elections in which there is only one party or only one candidate and in which showing up at the polls is mandatory evidently offer no choice. And even where real alternatives are present, such as in driving under or over the established speed limits, choice might be killed if the punishments are gross. Few could significantly choose if they knew that being caught a mile above the mark meant execution by a firing squad.

The fabric and the conditions of individual choice are excessively delicate. Parents who manipulate their child with dire threats and enormous rewards find it disappointing when he grows up with a will immobilized. They are amazed that, confronted with balanced alternatives perhaps for the first time, he is unable to think things through and to make up his mind. Deciding is an art learned by doing; the child who is given no opportunity to choose inevitably grows into a passive, aimless person. He might join the army or the church; his desire naturally puts him in the middle of a mediated chain, where he is relieved of the burden of thinking, choosing and feeling for himself.

Much of the legitimate impetus behind the desire of women to be liberated also derives from a common infringement of choice in the family. With children and an oppressively time-consuming home to tend, the scope of women's self-determination is radically reduced. This is exacerbated by the felt ineffectiveness of the wife. She has little influence on the central decisions that affect the location, welfare and future of the family; all of this is primarily determined by the circumstances of the breadwinner. In many cases, the final blow is the innocent attempt on the part of the husband to establish fiscal controls, or his desire to have a say in what she does with her time or in what she buys. The result is that women, many of whom have been brought up to make their own decisions or have learned to do this while working on their own, suddenly find themselves trapped. Deprived of autonomy, they feel coerced doing even those things which, given a choice, they would gladly do. Such a sense of being exploited and constrained frequently leads to an explosion in blind rage. Marriage partners who encroach on each other's autonomy soon live the storm this death of freedom brings. For often the loss of their freedom marks the end of their unstable troth.

I have tried to show that the thoughtless way in which we mouth each others' prejudices and opinions is a daily and enduring monument to mediation. For throughout much of my life others determine what I think and when. The fact that the direction, limits and even the content of my life are determined by decisions others make for me is evidence of the way a mediated world penetrates my innermost existence. Our feelings and great self-expressive acts are also not immune to this mediation. But in them we find even more explicitly a novel tendency which represents the final development of mediation in this sphere.

We find that others not only determine what form our self-expression takes or what we feel; on a growing number of occasions, they actually do the feeling and the self-expressing for us. There are traces of this even in the impact of others on our thoughts. For we do not mind having experts do our thinking for us. When they do our thinking, they have our thoughts for us. But normally, once they make up their minds as to what we shall believe, we at least actually go ahead and believe it; there is then still a residue of activity left in us. The peculiarity in the case of feelings is that frequently when someone feels on our behalf, we think of him as feeling in our stead. Similarly, when someone performs a self-expressive act for us, we often leave the matter at that, feeling no need of further self-expression.

The phenomenon of the President sending a man to have firsthand experience of a disaster or of the conduct of a war has become so common as to invite no further thought. We all agree it is commendable to want to get the perspective of the locals, to experience what the difficulties are. Yet it is revealing that the president sends another man to have the experiences *he* needs to have. Can the emissary report with any accurateness what he saw and smelled? Much of that never rises to explicit consciousness and hence cannot be readily put in words. The president has all the facts he needs; what he lacks is the sense of the immediacy of the scene. This is precisely what a deputized sense organ can never provide. Perhaps only poets should be sent on such missions: they know how to capture consciousness. Only their magic power can evoke a living mood through inanimate words, though even they can offer no substitute for immediacy.

The man who has my experiences can quickly turn into the person who undergoes my feelings. The function of those sad men and women who are sometimes hired to stand by graves heaving momentous sighs and rubbing their eyes red with handkerchiefs, is not to lead the mourning for the dead. They do the grieving in the place of the bereaved; their role is to externalize the pain. We are glad to have their visible suffering replace the invisible grief at death which gnaws at our hearts. There is more reluctance to surrender our feelings of a strong and positive kind. But it is not uncommon to find intermediaries even in our delight. We then enjoy only faded pleasure at the thought that someone is being pleased on our behalf.

The passive or impotent man might take vicarious delight in getting his wife to lay with some strong stud, as dogs stand around and watch the strongest mate. A great deal of the enjoyment we derive from movies is of the same sort. We see the hero's sufferings and joy, his victories at love, his broken hopes. We live through him without really feeling what he feels; we rehearse his life in image and in thought without undergoing it. The distance between film and audience is particularly poignant because in the back of our minds we all know that this is a story none now enacts, that these are the feelings of shadows, not of men. In the theatre, confronted by live actors, we might become engaged. We can get involved in the plot and rhetoric, and for the moment forget that these are actors and we see only a play. The actors themselves might assume their roles with vigor and in turn find that the character they play takes control of them. Then they begin to feel the sorrows of Oedipus or the noble outrage of Antigone.

There is nothing like this in the moviehouse. The scope of action here vastly outruns the narrow stage. Emotions can be enhanced almost at will: the closeup of a rugged face in pain is like turning up the amplifier until the sound envelops the entire body and there is no escape. Yet there is something unreal about it, at least partly because it is exaggerated, because it focuses only on the face and leaves out the rest of the body's response, because in the end what we see is only celluloid. Our response to two-dimensional shapes is very different from the response we make to living, moving persons. Pity and fear attack us more immediately in a play; in the movies few lips actually tingle when colored shadows kiss.

The popularity of movie magazines, romantic novels and books of adventure points to the same phenomenon. The lives of the people who figure in such fiction are replete with experiences we shall never have, with strong emotions and powerful huzzas. It is not that we have no feelings when we read such pulp. We have some mild pleasures and, when appropriate, distress on thinking or imagining what our heros feel. But our emotions clearly lack the scope and intensity of those we read about. Our feelings are not

107

even of the same sort as the feelings served up by fiction or hearsay to sate our appetites. In reading of the pain of losing child and home we experience fleeting discomfort, in picturing a moment-ous orgasm we feel but a moment's bittersweet delight. Vicarious pleasures are pleasures of the mind; they are faint, distorted echoes of the feelings of persons we imagine or observe.

One can find innumerable instances of the same tendency to have others feel and live for us throughout our culture. We turn to gourmets not only to tell us what tastes to look for and where. Most of us are satisfied to have them enjoy these subtle sensations for us, while we eat our hamburgers. People seem to take pride in declar-ing that they know little about good painting, fine music or even pleasant smells. "Let us leave this to the experts," they appear to say. "If these good things deserve appreciation," they might add, "we have our specialists to take care of that." We have not quite reached the stage where we surrender all of our pleasures to those who could deal with them with greater expertise and therefore perhaps even enjoy them more. Will the day come when we send our sweetheart a professional lover and she, in turn, provides her own substitute?

Implausible as this may sound, it is simply the physical rendition of what is already commonplace on the emotional plane. For frequently, our needs and interactions are shaped by television, movies and what we read. Even our moods are set by what the director presents and then the words and actions of the observed principals begin to function as our own. Watching a movie together, husband and wife communicate through the words spoken on the screen; they identify with the characters in the soap opera and can, therefore, remain personally bare. The actors already do the talking and the emoting on our behalf. Why should they not do all our private acts?

Within the family, the man has traditionally surrendered functions of feeling, sensitivity and emotional display to the woman. Many a father thinks it superfluous to hug or kiss his child, since the mother already does that. He cannot conceive it as his job to show how he feels or to respond to the need for love. The key notion here is that he cannot think it his *job*. The world of divided labor, of acts mediated on each others' behalf, of fragmented chains of action requiring specialized expertise has taken hold of, has in fact taken over, the inner life. And as the inner person falls to mediation, is stripped of feeling and personality, his self-expressive acts are given over to the outer world.

We then encounter a momentous paradox. Perhaps all of our acts reveal our personalities. But not everything we do is self-expressive. The self-expressive act flows naturally from who, what and where we are. Our hearts are poured into it and a deep satisfaction is the sure result. It is a song or shriek wrung from the soul, something that makes the man manifest. None can look from the outside and say that an action is or is not an expression of one's self. Often we ourselves fail to know. Spontaneous pleasure engendered by the action sometimes gives us a clue. At other times, we can actually sense the smooth naturalness of the act. The reason we often do not know is that the self is not a completed thing. It is perpetually in process: it becomes, grows and sometimes makes itself. Some of our acts, therefore, are prophecies of who we are to be: they become expressions of the self in retrospect. In being performed they create a self that matches them. This interdependence of the self and its acts, the dynamic interaction of what we do and who we are is the very process of creating a self.

Self-expressive acts, therefore, are not dispensable niceties. They are central to the life of every self as intimate conditions of its growth. The paradox is that these acts, which are intertwined with our being, are removed from the sphere of our agency and control. That which should flow as a natural consequence of who we are ceases to flow at all. Instead, we seize on some things that others do for us and substitute them as expressive acts. The self, then, does not express itself at all. The death of self-expression makes self-creation impossible, and since our personalities cannot exist without being renewed, we soon cease to be dynamic, flexible, thinking human beings. The self then becomes a glass filled with whatever liquid the world may provide. Instead of self-wrought acts to satisfy the soul, we seek nothing but peace and entertainment. Desire, like an octopus, stirs the waters for prey but we never move. For at the center where the storm should be, at the dead center, we are simply dead.

Our self-expressive acts in love and song have been surrendered long ago. A girl who had just returned from Europe once told me that the cathedrals and the museums did not impress her as much as the young people who on a Spanish afternoon had played their guitars near the fountain in the square. They had not played very well, but that did not matter. They had not played to please anyone, which seemed to make their song sweet and their joy spontaneous. Never had she seen happiness bubble from people the way water cascades from fountains or bursts from springs. It had not occurred to them to put on a record or to use the car radio to blast the silence of the square. The thought that they could make music and do the singing for themselves had been a revelation to her. It haunted her for weeks on her return.

Few of us are haunted by the possibility of giving vent to our own internal affections or of creating feelings by a rich expressive life. The day of the eccentrics who thought and felt and acted for themselves—unpredictably for others but with an inspired unity in their own eyes—is over. Even long ago, perhaps, they were rare exceptions to the norm. At any rate, today the overwhelming trend is to follow the trend, to be invisible in the mass, to be worry-free by being empty inside.

In an unrecorded conversation, God asked Jonah, "If you will not stand up for Me, who will do My work?" Each of us could ask the same question of himself. Who is to do the thinking, feeling, good living for me? The answer would be the same as what Jonah told God, hiding his face. He quietly whispered, "Anyone but I."

8 Mediated Remedies For Psychic Distance

Consciousness is a latecomer in life. Much of what happens to us, much of what we do never rises to explicit knowledge. Our bodies and our souls obey laws unconsciously. The embryo grows without a thought; it has much to teach the thoughtful embryologist. The psychological laws embodied in what we do are hidden from the gaze of the shrewdest Freud or Jung. Knowledge comes last, if it comes at all. The world operates without it well enough. We fly by instinct or by the seat of our pants, and if our subtle, unconscious sense is aligned to the movements of the world, we fly well and get where we want to go. The ideal of a scientific life, a life designed and controlled by conscious principles, is magnificent in its daring, but it is a dream. If we were gods, perhaps we could rule our lives. But since other gods are as unpredictable as other men, perhaps even then we would be open to contingency and chance, and in the end would have to resort to instinctual art.

We have little explicit consciousness of the extent of mediation and the attendant psychic distance in our lives. Many feel that all is not well, and almost everyone has experienced firsthand the misery of being empty and feeling impotent. Yet they may not know the source of emptiness, they do not suspect that the pain grew from impotence. Lack of knowledge rarely stops response. Their bodies and their souls have taken instinctive countermeasures. They have done what they could to combat the pain without knowing consciously whence it came or how the remedy worked.

Many of us do not know that we struggle daily to cure ourselves.

Just as mediation takes many forms, the urge to escape it is also omnimodal. The surburban gardener who, momentarily drunk with the pregnant smell of soil, tears off his gloves to feel the rich, wet ground is unconsciously in search of immediacy. He wants direct contact with the fertile, alluring reality of dirt. There is no metaphysic in his mind; it is simply that working the ground in gloves feels inadequate after a while. He senses that there must not be anything between him and the earth: he wants the sensuous feel, the grubby hands, the filth under the nails.

On a broader scale, much of the drug culture may be seen as an attempt to escape bland or secondhand experience. Evidently, anything as widespread as the drug craze that swept the country in the late 1960's must have complex conditions underlying it. There are always a multitude of causes. All generalization, therefore, is risky. The inner city resident who is on heroin to escape a life without possibilities is not to be classed with the children of suburbanites who try a little pot or LSD for the experience. But there is considerable evidence that at least among those for whom drugs are not an escape from oppressive economic conditions, hallucinogens fulfill the special purpose of enriching an otherwise impoverished experience.

Those who smoke pot on a habitual basis frequently report that it is only under its influence that they are able to feel and enjoy with the intensity they think proper to a human being. Music, tastes, smells, even the emotional subtleties of human interaction then loom larger than life. Objects stand out from their background with a vividness that makes the very act of perception a permanent joy. Feelings well up and overwhelm, laughter and crying become free, the entire body begins to function as a sense organ that resonates with the movements of the world.

Descriptions of this, couched in the language of grateful enthusiasm, reveal that many who try drugs have never managed to feel alive before. The drug of their choice enables them to overcome the inner emptiness due to internalized mediation. The thin stream of their sense life is quickened and given substance. They can reverse thereby, for at least an hour, the impact of a mediated world that leads to virtual sense deprivation.

Mescaline and LSD offer a different way of escaping the same mediation. Instead of merely sensitizing our organs so the world may come to call, they tend to create a world all their own. These drugs appear to provide what mediation makes impossible. They enable us to have thoughts and experiences our station does not allow. We can find ourselves in the shoes of someone else, living— for an eternal moment—his life, seeing the world as only he sees it. The desire to escape to such other worlds is understandable, given the narrowness of our own. The civil servant who pushes pen all day, whose life is weekday business and weekend waiting to resume his rounds, may well find his eyes opened by the first pill or soaked sugar cube. It is not surprising if he then spends his weeks earning a living, but in his own view lives only on weekends, in a happy trance.

Somber businessmen have testified to the power of these drugs, as though they bore witness to their god. To them the daily manipulation of things and people, the narrow grasp on nature through their role was perhaps never enough to sate the appetite. The world and their free intense lives in it were always there just beyond their grasp, vaguely adumbrated, uncertainly hoped for, longingly felt. The discovery of drugs gave them freedom and purpose. They did not become addicts or dropouts. They managed to keep a firm hold on their business and on the business of life: everything stayed on an even keel. Their new world was the private joy of evenings and weekend flings; whoever was denied a share of this part of their life never knew that they were not merely businessmen, never suspected the other realm in which they lived.

Those who stand against drugs by claiming that it is people or nature or God that turns them on are clearly suggesting important alternatives. Human relations and the omnicolored world could, in principle at least, sustain a lifelong high. But this requires immense and continuing internal effort. Faith perhaps is just the inner energy to live and to live to the hilt in the teeth of weakness and disaster. But this is not a real alternative for most of us. It involves a sharp realignment of our attitudes, a conversion not so much to some dogma or belief as to active self-directedness. Whatever formal conviction or belief is thought best to express it, faith in its essence is activity. It is best called faith-ing, the active conversion of vicissitudes into matter for growth and life and gratefulness.

In a world that creates and rewards passivity, faith and energy are rare or dying virtues. Those who want life and want it more abundantly turn to solutions consistent with passivity. To take a drug involves only movements, no activity. We need a few motions of the hand and mouth; the rest is done quietly by the alimentary tract. From then on it is like a private show; the fevered brain may work, but we can lean back and let the sensations roll over us without resistance or complaint. There is greater courage in the initial act of shooting up: here we have to pierce the body, do violence to our sacred self to get the sensations we hope that we desire. But soon even this becomes routine: the stinging pain of the needle no longer carries interest. Its meaning is gone and it becomes a mediating means to longed for passive joy.

The passivity that underlies drug-escape from mediation is clearest in the case of the young. For them roles are more limiting and oppressive than for older, settled people. They have not as yet found out who they are and what they want to do. A social structure that places young persons in restrictive roles early in life faces the risk of their restlessness and furtive experimentation. The full integration of the young into the social fabric presents a problem for every society. Few have the means and wisdom to allow the young a period of free experimentation, some years in which to try new lifestyles, act out enthusiasms, test the limits of their strength. Where the wisdom might have been present, the means were lacking and the young had to be integrated into the work force at an early age. We now have the means and the young show a great need for periods of personal trial and error. Yet we seem to lack the wisdom to let them make their own mistakes and learn for themselves which forms of life are simply not worth the cost. We half-consciously suppress and the entire mediated structure of modern society discourages active experimentation by the young. As a result, their explorations are internalized or driven underground. They try on roles, modes of life and odd sensations mainly through drugs in their private rooms.

There is something paradoxical about a society that can afford to keep the young out of the work force for an extended period of time and yet imposes ever more rigid structures on their schooling. The effort to ease our children into slots in our mediated chains leaves their lives regimented from kindergarten on. They find the world structured and ready for them when they arrive: even in their own lives little appears open to choice. They do not feel free to fail and hence never learn the joy of success. They are honed like fine instruments for social tasks. Teachers and parents both know that the key is to be like ball bearings, accommodatingly smooth. It is most important that no feathers get ruffled and no one is disturbed. To be active is a guarantee of being different and to be different spells trouble for adjustment. Adjustment is just another word for trouble-free adoption of roles, for fitting smoothly into mediated chains. With such purposiveness in our design of children, it is not surprising that they grow into empty adults who know not what they want. Having never had occasion to structure their own lives or to discover what they like, they dread their weekend and their open hours.

I once met an old woman who worked under excruciating conditions in a laundry. Her relief came through complaining, her joy by trivial gossip with others who worked there. I thought she hated her job. But a few days before her vacation in the spring she told me that she dreaded being away from the structured misery of her station. To be at home meant hours without content, shapeless mornings and insignificant nights. To her, freedom was boredom: having had no experience in autonomy and no knowledge of her needs, she never learned the skill to make life exciting. A student who once came to my office to discuss the course of studies he should pursue revealed the same effect of overstructuring. I suggested that one of the most important criteria for making his choice was to determine what he really liked. People tend to be good at what they like. I told him I thought it better to be good at a modest task one enjoys than to suffer misery as a miserable doctor. And then I asked him what it was he really liked to do. He had no idea. The very question surprised and bothered him: in nineteen years no one had asked him what he really liked or wanted, no one invited him to search his soul and see what he could find.

At least three reasons for drug-escape are clearly related to mediation. The first is to relieve the tension, the boredom, the palpable fragmentation that is the share of virtually everyone who earns a living, who occupies a role in a mediated chain. The second is to combat the passivity that inevitably follows fragmentation, constriction into roles and lodging the motive force for our acts in others who surround us. The third is to overcome the narrow scope and bland quality of sensory life which attends passivity. In each case the attempt is to use alcohol or other drugs to reduce our distance from others, from the real world, even from ourselves. Many of us feel with a quiet, unconscious desperation that we are not in close contact with anything. In abnormal cases the distance is so great that the mind floats away, out of touch with everything that pulses with reality. This is the state of the maddest among the organization men, human beings who neither see nor hear, just act on orders like controlled machines. For them everything that evokes pity or horror simply by being seen is disinfected of its feeling tone; their perception is in bondage to abstract ideas, ideologies.

Many of us who have not reached this stage have nevertheless gone far into the cocoon of the mediated world. The distance we feel from everything and everyone demands escape. With three martinis, with a puff or a pill, we can forget for a few hours or at least pretend that we forget. The tension dissolves, passivity gives way to elation, the senses become wet with excitement and are alive again. For the moment, human contacts seem free, our activities rich in meaning and the world immediate. Drugs destroy psychic distance, even though they do so only for the moment.

This short-lived bliss has itself as its fatal flaw. The bliss is good, but that it is short-lived is the source of endless pain. The ultimate problem is not the damage drugs do; one might well want to pay the cost if only their benefits were steady and sustained. But as a strategy for life drugs simply do not work: highs grow ever more difficult to sustain and, tragically, the very conditions of frequent escape deepen our dependence on reality. Drugs, then, represent no ultimate solution to the problems of mediation. For whatever relief we gain through them is itself achieved through a mediated act. The mediation is in this case subtle and physiological, but it is present nonetheless. The pill or the drink or the shot is but a mediating tool to change our consciousness.

The ultimate insufficiency of drugs resides in that they change our consciousness alone. They do not really eliminate our distance from each other and the world. Instead, they create a world of appearances and for a moment persuade us to believe that that is the reality we confront. But there is only appearance in this world and these appearances burst regularly in our face. Whatever we believe in our drunken moments, when we sober up we find that in reality nothing has changed. Our objective relations remain what they have been, the structure of our loneliness stands inviolate. We still find ourselves at a great remove from everything whose company we seek. Our passivity is, if anything, enhanced and we feel wrung out for having caught a glimpse of a better world only to learn that it is not ours to retain. Sometimes appearances can affect reality. But drug-induced euphoria offers no change and only the appearance of escape.

Addiction is the ultimate confession of impotence. The addict loves his simulated world, yet he knows real life can never be like that. He clings with desperation to his rosy glow: he can neither give up his happy world nor make reality rise to his ideals. The only solution is to opt for appearance and to deny the reality of what we all too painfully know to be the facts. Tacitly, the addict knows that drug mediated escape from psychic distance is no escape at all, for it leaves everything unchanged. It is this knowledge that he tries to suppress by the indefinite extension of his high. It is as if he thought that he can do nothing beyond pretending that his life is good and whole. Yet he cannot even pretend that without the help of mediating drugs.

The half-conscious urge to escape a passive and impoverished sense world shows itself also in a variety of other behaviors. The Casanovan heroic promiscuity that seems to have become commonplace might have its origin in this syndrome. It may well be that the reason for it is not to build one's ego or to degrade the opposite sex. There is a naive desire for knowledge involved in it: young people seriously entertain the possibility that after a hundred partners there is still something new to learn. They also find novelty and excitement in the chase; by contrast with such nomadic hunt, established relations are tediously predictable. Their hope thus is for enlarging the breadth and enhancing the vivacity of experience. And ultimately we all hope that physical intimacy will break down the psychic distance that separates us from one another. This is an attractive thought. How could one seriously believe that bodies which freely interpenetrate leave their souls untouched? Yet, by the cruelest paradox, bodies entwined leave minds separate and feelings detached. Sex as a way of getting to oneself through another is still an instance of mediation. One either cannot get to oneself that way at all, or on getting there finds the house empty and the hearth cold.

The desire to be entertained is also a direct result of passive emptiness. Reading takes a double activity: the eyes have to move along the lines and the imagination must reconstruct the heat of actions described in a cold medium. It is easier by far to exercise the eyes alone and even then to leave them largely passive by shifting the burden of motion to the lively screen. It is for good reason that television frequently puts us to sleep: unless the program engages the mind, the watcher is as near total passivity as a person awake and well can conceivably be. It is only a small step from there to be lulled to sleep: the play of colors, the inoffensive voices from the box slip us insensibly over the threshold into quiet night. Television relaxes us, it winds us down. Since it requires nothing of us, we can let go. If sleep follows, we can at least be sure that we have missed nothing and get some rest without the need for pills.

But this is sleep, not entertainment, although in current programing the difference is hard to tell. The paradigm of entertainment is for people to sing and joke merrily, to carry on while we watch at a distance, calm or mildly bored. The job of the entertainer, presumably, is to divert our attention from our daily cares, to cheer us or to show a world of happy make-believe. Satisfaction comes from the pleasant union of passivity and identification with the active actors. Excitement, achievement, adventure can all be had by simply keeping the eyes open; if aggression has to be released, one can watch football or turn to wrestling late at night.

By identification with what goes on in the show, for a moment we can make ourselves believe that we are active. Involvement in the action might show in suppressed body movements, in muscle tensions and in flashings of the eye. In this way, passivity yields a simulacrum of action, a passive or suppressed activity, a moment of frozen motion. And since one aim is to expand experience beyond the narrow limits allowed in daily life, the more bizarre the entertainment, the better. Variety shows capitalize on this and bring us an endless string of one-man bands, octogenarians who play the Star-Spangled Banner on wine glasses, trained seals that can respond with honks to the deepest questions. The truly weird is no longer the specialty of horror shows; it has come to inhabit prime time and prime location in all the media. Entertainers are more likely to succeed if they have an element of gross uniqueness to play up; midget gunslingers, overgrown men who sing falsetto, Ph.D.'s who claim to talk to plants are assured of instant success.

The motive throughout is to shock our bland perceptual life. To accomplish this, we resort to visual paradoxes, to the presentation of the strange. Animals are trained to act and look like human beings: dogs wear skirts and curtsy, horses count, elephants wash windows, monkeys blush. By a strange inversion, humans are made to look and act like animals. On give-away shows they scream like apes, beg like starving dogs or stand transfixed in front of new refrigerators the way mice are paralyzed when a snake appears.

But the expansion of consciousness these odd experiences bring is itself mediated and artificial. Much of the strangeness we see is trivial: it makes no difference to life to know that seals can play the French horn or that John Wayne can stop all crime in the imaginary West. The excitement over action read about or seen on the screen is itself synthetic and without result. It is all a matter of the imagination, like hugging a pillow or feeling one's steamy member in a private room. Real action still resides in others, or perhaps in no one at all; in any case, no one is left improved after the show. We may feel relieved or pleased at seeing the story come to a good end, but psychic distance is not removed thereby. It is, once again, suspended for a moment in the mind, only to return in an hour more intensely or, at best, unchanged.

But the function of entertainment, rightly conceived, is precisely this momentary relief. It suspends the inner emptiness, fills the void with pleasant images. We feel aglow, alive, aflutter with good thoughts; none of the instant pleasure is rendered invalid by the fact that it will soon be gone. Pain, distance, the threatening strangeness of the world are set aside; let them return, if they will, but in the meantime life can run its course. Pleasure flows freely, the world of appearances is, for the moment, believed. It is a tribute to the power of entertainment that many people have chosen it as their ultimate escape. They have trained themselves to feel little during the day; their evening escape is not in drugs or drink, but in being entertained. The empty soul is filled with song at night; talk of it fills the next day with meaning. Anticipation of the weekend becomes not the hope for free time with family or friends, but longing for the next episode in the series, for specials or an awards telecast.

Television offers the most potent mediated relief of psychic distance. Its function is not only to provide instant and continuous entertainment. It can be put in the service of knowledge and education. And it can place us directly in touch with what happens on the other side of the world. The power of the electronic medium is immense: those who maintain that one of the main reasons why the Vietnam war became unpopular was the treatment it received on the evening newscast, may not be far wrong. The pictures shown, the sounds recorded, the nuanced meanings of the commentators all conspired to create an image of senselessness and horror. War is never pretty, but it has never before been played in color in fifty million dens and living rooms.

At its best, television can get the audience involved in a way no newspaper account or radio review could ever do. Part of the reason for this is the dominance of our eyes and the direct connection they have with our feelings. This is enhanced by the fact that television is a multi-media instrument: it assaults the ears at the same time that it titillates the eyes. As a result, it can reach out and pull us into itself until the room in which we sit, the reality of our everyday surroundings, recede into nothingness. All that remains is the screen and what it reveals. And soon it is a screen no more: the action seems directly there or we seem transported to the far-off place where it is occurring. In this way, television appears singularly well equipped to overcome distance. It bridges the space between my living room and the rest of the waning world. It transports me into the past and future without my having to leave the room. The psychic distance that separates me from my acts and from the consequences of what, unknowingly perhaps, I help to cause recedes or disappears.

If television were well used, it could do a great deal to counteract the consequences of mediation. It has the potential to be the single most effective instrument of mass education. Under its influence, the distance created by extended chains of mediation shrivels like plastic touched by heat. Within minutes after the act, we may observe a palpable demonstration of what flows from it. In this way, the elaborate conditions of our daily life can be exposed. We can be taken from electric generating plant to strip mining in the flicker of an eye; within seconds we can see harsh chemicals leached from the abandoned rock, poisoned waters and sulphur-laden air. Everything can be laid before us effectively and fast, ready for absorption, waiting for public choice.

Imaginative use of television could revolutionize democratic processes, as well. The citizen can be transported into the inner councils of government, he can be made to feel that he is present at the deliberations of his representatives. Coverage of the Watergate hearings has done a great deal to bring the people closer, at least for awhile, to the political processes of the nation. Coverage of key debates in the House and the Senate, even in state legislatures and in city councils, could well provide the sense for all that they determine their own fate through the government.

The periodic assemblies of the people advocated by Rousseau are impossible in a large industrial state. But something like them may well be realized by the extensive use of television, feeding instant information from each local group to all. Even the suggested hook-up of voting machines with television sets is not without some merit. It would enable us to have our opinions heard instantly. The value of it would reach beyond the convenience of having a machine on hand for straw votes and public opinion polls. It might establish the television set as an instrument for universal communication. It could enhance our participation in the political process and through that in all the affairs of our complex world.

Public education must not be conceived in a narrow way. It is not restricted to lectures on Hamlet or scholarly programs on the life of Leonardo. Sesame Street educates with no sacrifice of humor or entertainment. Adult programs could be no less instructive, if only creative thought went into conceiving them. And even as things are, it is not that existing adult programs fail to teach us things: practices are laid out inviting imitation, lessons get taught, values are endorsed. The only problem is that the practices are useless or harmful and frequently the values are anti-social. The issue is not that in police stories crime is shown to pay. The end may be moralistic as a matter of convention or routine; that is not what engages our feelings. The message may be independent of the story line: attention is on the details of the crime, the gusto of the chase, the romance of the life of criminals. Their unhappy ending is thrown in or perceived as an afterthought; it is certainly not enough to outweigh the fascination of a fast and easy life. Achilles was offered the choice between a long, tedious existence and a short but glorious career. He chose to live high and went out in a blaze. Little beyond fear and indolence stops each of us from choosing the same.

Perhaps the real problem with television today is that it teaches useless skills. The values it endorses are not conducive to personal satisfaction. The only thing that keeps the devotees of the tube from acting out lives of crime and decadence is the infinite passivity it casts on all who worship at its shrine. Like some cruel god, it presents entrancing possibilities, though only at the cost of freezing the will and killing all our motives. The result is that television becomes a medium of wish fulfillment, like a dream, in which we gain only imaginary release.

The classic visible manifestation of this was widely publicized during the Washington, D.C. riots in the middle 1960's. At the height of the looting and burning, two men drove up to a furniture store and carried the largest color television set through the broken window to their waiting car. Their desire was not for weapons or for food. They had no interest in action or ideology. All they wanted was a good set to take home so they could watch the riots with a frosty beer. A nation of television watchers has little reason to fear a revolution.

The most evident place on television where continued useful education takes place is the evening newscast. Here the value of the electronic medium is immense: it can put us in instant contact with what goes on around the globe. In fact, most of us know little about the world beyond our immediate neighborhood that is not brought to us by newspaper or television. The mechanisms of rumor and of individuals bearing news of changes in the distant world have been displaced by the formal media. Our dependence on them is almost total; as a result, their deliverances are difficult to criticize. Written accounts in newspapers can at least be re-read and analyzed. But television stories are heard and they are gone, and the pictures they show us command instant assent. Perceptions are trusted in a way no word can ever be. If the image looks authentic, we soon think we see the real thing; in an unguarded moment, we might even think that we are there.

In this way, television accounts acquire a sense of full reality. They advance from mere stories to supplements to our real world; eventually they become partial substitutes for it. Continuing reports from a distant battlefield may soon give us the feeling that we are there participating in the decisions and the action. A well done visual report of some local tragedy can function as an acceptable substitute for going to see it. Observing others help the victims becomes an adequate alternative to going to help them ourselves. Ultimately we reach the stage where we can simply see no difference between physical presence and the visual narrative television provides. If anything, we think the television account preferable. For one, the cameraman has a location vastly superior to any we could command. For another, we sit comfortably in our living room and feel relieved of having to put up with the smell and the crush of the crowd.

In this way, television becomes a substitute for life. The image takes the place of reality, pure perception usurps the place of action. Here mediation has come full circle: having wrenched the world away from us, it now returns it as an image on the screen. The marvel of this mediated cure for psychic distance is that at its best it manages to pass itself off as the real thing. Drugs and entertainment smell of unreality; they may expand our experience and give us the sense that distances can wane, but they are confessedly momentary and thoroughly unreal. They are bubbles that reveal alternative worlds and then burst. No one for long believes that these worlds endure, no one is fooled into supposing that drug insights or bizarre stories disclose the substance of the world.

This, in the end, is the difference between them and the evening news: just as no one believes that entertainment reveals the world, so no one denies that newscasts do. The evening news then becomes our peephole on the world; the magic tube in the room functions as a crack in the wall through which the world reports itself to us. The most remarkable fact this engenders is diminished psychic distance without increased activity. We sit, more passive then ever, and all we do it watch. Yet we seem to have firsthand contact with reality: we hear the rumble of earthquakes, we see the ocean swallow boats and fishing village on the African coast. The sense of reality this generates is so great, the sense of immediacy so compelling that we forget the ultimate secret of the tube. All of this is image and illusion: it is a replica of reality brought to life by the human eye and mind.

Some empiricist philosophers maintain that the world consists of experiences. For them, the ultimate reality is perception and its object. As a result, they cannot distinguish action from our perception of it. And since the objects of sense exist passively as and when they are perceived, real activity is restricted to the internal, invisible will and to perceiving itself. George Berkeley thought that something like this was true; he persuaded himself that the body was the image we have of it, that physical action was simply our perception of the act. The entire world thus becomes a momentous sensory illusion. To make it seem more real, Berkeley introduced God as the source of it. God, then, pipes perceptions into our soul, as though they were music by Muzak. Better yet, Berkeley's world is the world of the news telecast. Imagine the tube stretching from wall to wall, with a continuous newscast day and night. Images surround us while we watch. There is no world beyond these walls, the newscast reports no external facts: what you see of it is all there is anywhere. The story is both report and reality, a report reporting itself, a reality created for the telling and in the show.

This idea of a world of pure perception was made electronically possible by the invention of television. But the television world suffers from the same weakness Berkeley could never overcome. There is a real difference between the perception of action and the real act. This is not well appreciated by sense-empiricists: it is understandable that to perception there is no such difference. But the moment we agree that the real world is not one of appearances only, perceived action becomes but photograph, a frozen image of dynamic acts.

If there is a gap between engaging in action and perceiving it, there is a momentous gulf between engaging in action and perceiving the *image* of an act. It is only the image we see on television, the act is removed and probably no longer exists. It may never have existed in the context and with the meanings that come to us. For there is a crucial and insurmountable difference between seeing the image through the media and actually being there to see. The analysis of the difference has to begin with the disparity between involvement of the eye through a twenty-three inch patch and involvement of the whole body and person in a three-dimensional way. Real situations envelop us, they penetrate the body in subtle and insensible ways. In a real, though only half-conscious way, the entire body is a sense organ that responds to the exigencies of the situation. All the senses are engaged: we see and smell and touch concurrently. Much of what we perceive fails to rise to explicit consciousness, yet all of it is registered and stored. All contributes to the feeling tone that surrounds and shapes our ultimate response.

One feels embarrassed at having to make a point as evident as this. Yet the omnipresence of images in our society and our commitment to passive perception tend to make us forget the difference between act and illusion, between body and our picture of it. Reliance on televised accounts robs us of total participation, of immediacy that seeps in through the pores. What we see is determined by the cameraman. We cannot turn our heads to see what others in the crowd look like or how they might respond. What the camera focuses on is larger than life; it is wrenched out of context and becomes the only thing happening, anywhere.

Actual presence presents a different picture. To be sure, there is a wrecked car at the scene of the accident and there is a crowd. But we have no close-up of the blood on the front seat, no doting presentation of smoke out of the ruined engine. Being on the spot, we can see the green grass and the sky above, catch a spectator's hungry look at the torn skirt of a pretty passenger. To the person there, all is in context, all is interaction. Involvement is a natural result; hope, revulsion, heartrending pity, the entire machinery of our affective life is immediately engaged.

Television presents the distant scene. Psychic distance can be reduced in this way. The scope of consciousness can be expanded, indifference can, to some extent, be overcome. But in transporting distant events to the living room, the benefit of real presence is lost. The circumstances, bereft of natural texture and structure, lose much of their affective tone. In the process of mediation through persons and electronic machines, what rendered the circumstances human and vital drops out. We are left with a visual simulation that leaves us dry. The very mediation that brings the distant here, kills it in the process of conveyance. What we have in the end is a thin slide to examine under the microscope, not the large Australian worm of which it once was part. Mediated remedies yield relief, but they do not cure. Their effectiveness presupposes the mechanism of the disease. In the process of making us feel better, they perpetuate the malady.

9 A Cure For
Psychic Distance

The man whose body harbors deadly lumps, whose organs are eaten by cancer may know nothing of his ailment. He might feel discomfort or some pain; he may be depressed from time to time. A gray pall might descend on his private moods and yet he may be ignorant of the causes of this change. By the time he presents himself to his doctor and is diagnosed, it is too late. In the light of his new knowledge of the end, so much of what he had not noticed or could not understand falls into place. In retrospect, he can see it all and only grieves that he had done nothing for so long.

The advantage of the cancerous man is that at least he can be diagnosed. There are examinations and biopsies, there are clinical tests and chemical analyses. By contrast, the science of society is in its early stages. We cannot even tell the difference between a sick society and a healthy one. There is little agreement between diagnosticians as to ailment or remedy. The diseases imputed are frequently absurd or fanciful. An account of what is wrong with our lives typically reveals more about the person offering it than about the facts. Here everything is a function of the values and beliefs of the social critic.

We have no clear standards of sickness in society. Yet it is clear that not everything is well. Like the cancerous organism, we experience distress. There are pains and maladjustments, our unhappiness rises like gray smoke. For all the daily joys of life, the world's mood is somber. Our own society is torn by the self-doubt of sickness or of middle age. It is not true that everything is bad; it is not true that life has lost its zest. Joy and energy renew themselves forever; they stand up defiantly even in the teeth of death. But the fact that everything is not lost does not imply that all goes as it should, that human life has attained the satisfaction we crave. On the contrary, we have created a world of comfort and yet fulfillment has not followed suit. Control of nature, relative protection from the vicissitudes of fortune have not proved enough to make us satisfied.

The physical and social value of an industrial world must not be underrated. People today cannot even guess the misery that would come if our daily amenities were denied us or were given up. Yet the industrial world has put us in a cocoon. Mediated society has all but abolished direct contact with the world. We have been stripped of meaningful activity, our inner lives resemble a fading TV set. Our experiences come as though through gloves: everything real is distanced from our receptors by an unfeeling medium. We are far removed from our roots and acts; the consequences of our agency and of agents acting on our behalf seem alien or altogether beyond our ken. In a mediated world not even contact between cooperating humans remains immediate. For we do not work for and with each other as rounded persons. Instead, we fill roles in mediated chains; we touch each other largely in these roles. Thus human contacts themselves are restricted in scope and mediated through gigantic institutions.

These institutions appear to be beyond the control of any individual or group. Even the owners, rulers and elected heads find themselves in a social machine they cannot run; they become enmeshed in a structure that has its own momentum and creates its own constraints. What Hegel boldly called the cunning of reason, the hidden rationality that emerges from the apparent passion and disorder of the world, is now more appropriately seen as drift. To combat the cruel or aimless flux of structures requires a further edifice—central government—which creates even greater drift. In a world thoroughly bureaucratized and converted in the image of mediated man, everything natural and direct recedes to the far periphery. In the end, we may find ourselves as a whole generation of humans did in a tragic science fiction story. After all the animals were gone, their consolation was to watch the last living tree on television in their barren rooms.

The situation we face is delicate. Mediation not only provides a comfortable and safe existence for most of us. It is an unavoidable condition of life in a populous world. There can be no question of giving it up or of minimizing it. With its diminution would go a drop in comfort, in quality of life. A substantial curtailment of mediation would lead directly to a decrease in work opportunities and a deterioration of commercial, industrial and social ties. It would eliminate the conditions necessary for a large population and eventually return human existence to a horrid, primitive level. Mediated mass production is an indispensable condition of life for the masses; without mediation we would soon be reduced to monks singing dry songs in the wilderness.

But mediation exacts a price. The more comfortable we get, the farther we are removed from one another and from ourselves. How can we retain the benefits of mediation and eliminate or substantially reduce the psychic distance which is its greatest cost?

I have already discussed a number of specific strategies. Distance from our ends can be reduced by converting some or many of the things we do into activities which are valuable in and of themselves. We can strive for wholeness in our lives by refusing to be defined and exhausted in our roles. We can learn the consequences of the acts we help to perform and revise the rules of accountability so that all of us in mediated chains become more ready to take responsibility for our acts.

Government itself can be run in a fashion likely to decrease psychic distance. To do so, its primary aim must be the education in freedom of its citizens, and its procedures must be open, fair and participatory. There is some hope even in our internal life, if only we can take an active hand in shaping our thoughts and expressing our feelings.

All of these strategies share the common element of reestablishing a measure of immediacy in the world. In creating a complex social life, mediation does not destroy the possibility of appropriating and understanding it. A rich experience and warm sensory life become difficult to achieve but not impossible. They must be fostered consciously and with care. Their development cannot be left to good fortune or to chance.

The enhancement of immediacy and the enrichment of experience are possible only if they become explicit social goals. Individuals must be taught to seek and opportunities must be provided for achieving immediate exposure to a wide variety of experiences and activities. We already have institutions designed to accomplish this, at least to some extent, in the form of the educational system. Of course, if the provision of a broad spectrum of experiences is to be one of its foremost objectives, our method of education has to undergo significant changes.

There is a great Western tradition according to which the answer to all our ills is education. A rationalistic prejudice usually accompanies this view: the education is supposed to speak directly to the mind. If only reason could be enlisted in the service of life, so the argument goes, human practices would become enlightened and interactions would grow benevolent. Liberal education is typically thought to be the proper means for accomplishing this end. Since words are supposed to be the native medium of reason, liberal education has traditionally been confined to talk.

The rationalistic assumption that simply by talking to people we can turn them around is one of the more momentous illusions in the history of human thought. If we were disembodied souls aflutter with conclusions and evidence, better understanding would quickly make us act. But we are creatures of emotion and desire; our motives rise from the depths of bodies whose secrets we fail to understand. Words have an impact only when attached to this body of emotions, when they engage the interest of the creature. If there is no clear contact with the life of our feelings, with the desires that shape our lives, words become mere verbiage— endless, useless talk.

This is what has happened to the liberal arts. To gain the distance necessary for understanding, they have learned to move in a cold verbal medium. In philosophy, in literature, in the history of the arts, everything can be discussed, though little is ever felt. The student is given mounds of information. He is flooded with critical theories, his mind is invited to consider myriad alternative accounts. He is assured that all of this is relevant to life, that he can make no rational decisions without knowing these principles and knowing how to apply them. Yet he is never taught to apply them in real situations. The nearest he gets to reality is in classroom casuistry, in empty and abstract descriptions of moral problems.

At the same time, the student finds that his daily life goes on unabated. There decisions are made constantly, perhaps on principles we do not understand, but in any case in a way that is not enlightened by the classroom talk. It is not long before everyone learns the cruel truth: what goes on at home, in the world and in the dorms is real life, what goes on in the classroom is a game. Each course-game has its own language and rules which can be mastered in a week, or just before examinations in two nights. In a curious way, verbal mastery of this abstract knowledge is correlated with success in later life. The correlation is not natural: it is not that by learning what the liberal arts can teach us we live better and hence succeed as human beings or as citizens. Instead, it is one established by decree. Those who have gone to school for the longest possible time are declared to be superior: we give them opportunities no one else can have. Society appears committed to rectify the mistakes of educators; the intrinsic uselessness of a liberal education is compensated for by making it a condition of admission to special jobs and polite society.

Yet the students are not fooled. The more earnest among them are confused, the callous simply laugh and go their way. The confusion comes because they take their teachers seriously. They believe that what they learn should make a difference to how they live. But they do not find that it makes a difference and to their ultimate dismay they soon discover that it never made a difference to their teachers. Teachers and professors then stand unveiled as hacks who merely profess, as minor officials of the mediated world whose job is to hand on verbal culture, that is, to teach us how to talk.

The discovery is bewildering to the serious student. Wholeness of being requires unity of feeling and thought. Yet while reason is educated, feelings are allowed to go their merry way. Human faculties become detached from each other; often they pull in opposite directions. Reason cannot give guidance, emotions cannot render us humane or fertilize our thoughts.

The result is a crisis, frequently observed in better students.

The solution to it takes the form of surrender. Education then is no longer thought to be important. The focus shifts to enjoyment, to making money or to scholarship. In each of these cases, it is no longer supposed that the liberal arts bear much relation to life. Books may continue to be read, a vigorous philosophical argument may still be enjoyed, but these become isolated incidents. They are done, as the scholar proudly announces, for their own sake. This sounds like a mighty justification, conferring on insignificant talk all the dignity of an intrinsically valuable act. And there is little doubt that from time to time shafts of joy shine through the drudgery. But, for the most part, the claim that knowledge is an end in itself is a flimsy excuse for irrelevance.

In spite of the rationalistic assumption that underlies the current practice of the liberal arts and the self-wrought irrelevance that is its result, the only hope for systematically reducing psychic distance is education. But in order to make the difference it needs to, education itself has to be different from what it is today. It has to escape the narrow specialization imposed upon it in a mediated world. It must break down the boundaries between the physical sciences, the social sciences and the humanities. It must reach out of the classroom and invade every part of the community. It must, in fact, convert the entire society into a classroom and adapt its processes to educational use. In the end, it must eliminate the sharp distinction between education and daily life. Only in that way can it rationalize daily practice, improve our world and in the process fulfill its own promise of being a guide for life.

Teachers in the humanities have looked with envy at the success of professional education. It is not that nursing schools, law schools and engineering departments do such an impeccable job of educating. On the contrary, they suffer as much from shabby teaching and the emphasis on irrelevant facts as any college or high school curriculum. But by a strange alchemy, students in professional schools find themselves engaged by the material they study. A seriousness pervades learning in law school that even the most successful liberal arts course cannot match. In spite of all the complaints about poor teaching and narrow curriculum in medical schools, students there soon find themselves absorbed in the material. The reasons are evident. Students in these fields see their education as laying the groundwork of their future professional careers. But even more importantly, their curriculum encompasses both the abstract and the concrete; they learn both facts and skills. All the theories to which they are exposed are quickly converted into practice; everything conceptual makes a vital and lasting difference. The valued products of these fields—sound bridges, healthy people and protected rights—somehow permeate and shape the learning process. The goals manifestly demand skills for their achievement, the skills naturally require protracted practice and intelligent application of principles. As a result, theory and practice seem integrally connected in the professional schools. The danger there is not that of abstractness, but of robot-like reliance on practice alone. This may show itself in programming invariant responses or teaching mere skills without understanding, as in the high school shop.

Even education in the sciences has the benefit of a practical component. Work in the laboratory has a vivifying effect on the learning process. The problem is that in physics and chemistry, even in biology, the results to be achieved in the student lab are known well ahead. Consequently, laboratory work tends to become mechanical; frequently students who cannot achieve the desired effect pretend that they did. Since the learning has no expected impact beyond the classroom or the lab, little significance is attached to getting everything right. I remember dissecting a fetal pig in high school many years ago. When no one at the table could find the kidneys after a couple of attempts, we simply decided that we had found them and drew a pretty picture of them from a book. The point is that it made no difference whether we saw them or not; the ultimate motive was not knowledge for enlightened future actions but a grade.

Humanities education lacks even the minimal exposure to reality provided by the lab. If teachers could discuss how principles of their choice had changed their lives, there would be at least a breath of fresh air in the room. But scholars frown upon such merely practical or confessional activities. Teachers must keep themselves at a remove, convert reality into an impoverished description of it and deliver learned disquisitions on how to live. Even the grossest contradictions between one's life and the principles one teaches are acceptable. Since the teacher is supposedly the neutral vehicle of eternal wisdom, his own life is irrelevant to what he professes: we are supposed to listen to what he says and overlook his actions. The most eloquent proponents of wisdom lead degrading, fractured lives. Current education is based on the rule that we must disregard their own private assessment of their wisdom. If we did not, we might be led to ask the disabling question of why they do not buy what they are so ready to sell.

There is a central change that must occur in education, if it is to be effective in combating psychic distance. It must cease to be separated from daily life. The prevailing conception, which shows itself as early as the kindergarten years, is that living is one thing, education another. This is a fallacy that provides a comfortable living for many a manufacturer of educational toys. The notion they thrive on is that the ordinary objects of daily life are not sufficiently edifying for our children. Instead, special objects must be designed and marketed, which can be certified by educational experts as wholesome and thought-provoking. It is amazing that parents never learn the uselessness of these expensive gadgets from the contempt with which their children treat them. Instead, they read the desire of the child to play with spoons, cracker boxes and father's shoes as the expression of a distorted nature or of an early wish to avoid the benefits of learning. If fact, of course, the opposite of this is true. The child is naturally anxious to learn, and he learns best by imitating the important people in his life. Objects his mother and father would never think of using are below his contempt. By contrast with "educational toys," the ordinary things around the kitchen and the living room have an excitement, life and dignity of their own. By manipulating them, the child learns and grows in self-assurance.

The separation of education from life is institutionalized by providing special places where it can take place and special people who are experts at bringing it about. It is understandable that the school becomes an oppressive structure in the eyes of many students. Whatever delight they experience there derives from the occasional play allowed and the friendship of their peers. There is little pleasure left in the official learning process itself precisely because it is unrelated to anything a young and growing person perceives as important. Teachers fail to help matters much. Their training is in some field whose authenticated facts they are prepared to dispense unceasingly through the year. If they have had training in "education," they have a few scraps of current gossip about the human psyche, along with some conscious skills or tricks on how to teach. But given the initial separation of school and life and the rigid strictures on what and how to teach, even this background is inadequate to command the attention of a class. Children have an instinctive sense for the insincere and the boring; their natural defense in the schools is to fail to learn.

The ultimate failure of education is assured by the attitude of the parents. In the classic tradition of the mediated world, they think themselves relieved of the task of educating their children. They pay dearly, they say, to provide the best specialists for their offspring. To maximize educational benefits, they ship their children off to school at the earliest possible moment—in some cases before the age of two—and keep them there for the longest possible time each day. Even religious education has gone this way: learning in the family context has been supplanted by formal Sunday School sessions and vacation Bible schools. The point is that such formal education is conceived not as a supplement to what goes on in the home, but as a substitute for it. It may well be that the ultimate tragedy of mediation is not that we give up framing our own opinions, feeling our own feelings and creating our own personality, but that we relinquish the task of teaching and forming our children. To abandon self-creation is to assure the failure, in human terms, of this generation. To abandon the education of our children is to surrender hope for shaping the future. It is the ultimate confession of impotence.

If education is to be a force in life, it must be interwoven with all the activities of living. The world and our own natures are the great masters that teach us how to live; but even the greatest masters need attentive pupils. We are by nature alert animals: the world is our shell, our home, our hope. The first task of education is to retain this natural curiosity. For this reason, education cannot occur by dumping large bodies of fact and principle on unprepared victims. It must proceed when and where the occasion makes room for it, invites it or even requires it for better understanding.

Every change in life is an opportunity for teaching some lesson; instruction that proceeds without such natural context and occasion rarely succeeds.

Organic chemistry is an important and fascinating field. Questions and problems that only it can resolve arise in our lives daily. If learning it could be organized around circumstances when such problems come to the fore, the material would seem easy and the lessons unforgettable. As it is, a course in organic chemistry is experienced by most students as overwhelmingly dormitive or brutally hard. In college, such courses have come to serve as a device for the early screening of candidates for medical school. A great deal of instruction at all levels of schooling functions in a similar way; its primary purpose or result is not to help the understanding but to test the endurance and the concentration of students.

But, it might be objected, it is obvious that formal education must have a structure. We cannot wait for opportunities to arise before instruction in a field begins. We cannot count for continued interest in learning on a steady stream of problematic real situations. Universal and extensive education cannot be rendered hostage to contingent circumstances that may not come along. This is certainly true. But it is not a serious objection to what I advocate. The reason for this is twofold. First of all, we must not take a rigid or hysterical attitude about the quantity of knowledge we must cover in formal education. The spread and balance of the offerings in schools is praiseworthy. But there is little reason to demand that each person who graduates from high school or college should be acquainted with a fixed body of English literature or with optics or with the principles of devising questionnaires. Such insistence on "distribution requirements" or breadth of coverage is the last respects we pay to the notion of the generally educated or "Renaissance" man. As all last respects, it makes us feel better without accomplishing anything.

Moreover, opportunities for education are present more frequently than we care to acknowledge. The key is for teachers to be sensitive to the conceptual issues actuality perpetually opens. Without such sensitivity, our lives are full of missed opportunities. And, in any case, there is no reason to wait for circumstances to arise. If education and daily life are constructively interwoven, instructional opportunities can be produced by the learning process itself. To accomplish this, we must move the process away from its sterile isolation in the classroom. Ideally, the entire community ought to be the classroom for the young. By utilizing the resources of the community at large, educational opportunities can be created at will and incorporated into the learning process to enrich it and to render it relevant.

What we must do is nothing as bland or halting as the introduction of interdepartmental work. Breaking down artificial departmental barriers between chemistry and physics, between philosophy and sociology, between all adjoining fields, contributes to our appreciation of the interconnectedness of all knowledge. But while we remain on this level, we still deal only with knowledge of a conceptual sort. We neglect education of the senses and of the emotions and, most important of all, we fail to provide opportunities for the integration of all the human faculties which are involved in knowledge and action. It is this failure that makes it possible for human beings to claim to know something and yet to lack the slightest tendency to act on it. We must find a way to transcend mere verbal or conceptual knowing. Such cognition is central for understanding our condition and for improving it. But it is not enough. In the fullest sense, knowledge must have intelligent action not only as its accidental by-product but as its source and goal. It must arise from life and action and in the end find its fulfillment in them.

This is the reason why we must go far beyond the limited goal of breaking down the departmentalization of knowledge. We must reconceive the entire process of learning. First of all, the localization of the educational process must be overcome. Schools and classrooms must not be treated as shrines at which we worship laws and facts. There may well be a need for quiet places to think and talk, but to limit education to the classroom is to isolate it from its most effective instruments. The community in which the school is located throbs with life: in it we can find instances of every law and practice. To think that learning can be effective without direct personal, even physical, exposure to the living context of problems and activities is grievously to misunderstand the action-directed essence of the mind. Our senses grasp at once what we can never describe; our feelings are moved by what we see in a way they cannot be by words or theorems.

Here, again, professional education has been nearer the mark than the liberal arts. Medical students serve in the emergency room and rotate through every service in the hospital. Engineering students alternate courses and practical work. There is a desperate need for the same combination of theory and pratice in the liberal arts, for the same sustained thrust to have the learning process encompass both school and community. But we have to go beyond even what the professional schools currently do. For their interest is in teaching practical skills, in training people to assume definite places in mediated chains. The liberal arts must attend not to the development of skills for the performance of special tasks, but to the development of the person as a whole. This means that education from kindergarten through college and beyond must be the education of senses, emotions and character no less than of the mind.

As formal education expands its location, it also necessarily enlarges the teaching resources available to it. Schools of business have learned long ago that the practicing businessman is as valuable to their educational enterprise as the theorizing specialist on the faculty. It is not that the theorist fails to know in the abstract what the businessman lives through every day. But the vivid immediacy of living through it is one thing, abstract knowledge of it another. The businessman brings a rich practical perspective to the students which no professor, without that background, can provide. Similarly, if other fields expanded their educational efforts to encompass the entire city, all those engaged in the practice of what teachers teach would themselves become teachers of the young.

This would serve two important functions. Students could learn how principles are applied. They would gain a firsthand appreciation of the obstructions daily life puts in the way of clear vision and of all the practical difficulties of shaping the world to conform to human desires. This healthy infusion of reality into the life of reason would be matched by thought and reflection invading practice. The presence of students throughout the city would motivate people absorbed in unreflective lives to think about their condition. Critical questioning by the young would tend to keep daily activities from becoming routine. In addition, each day they would carry the stimulation of ideas, new theories and a potently innocent idealism to all those who have thought themselves too busy to attend to such matters.

If every person could view himself as making a contribution to the instruction of the young, the entire time scope of the educational enterprise would change. Schools and universities have on occasion made half-hearted attempts to move into adult education. In spite of these ventures, motivated more by greed and local pressure than idealistic convictions about the need for continued learning, it is clear that we think of education as a process that can be finished in a finite period, considerably before our demise. Its completion is celebrated by graduations and the conferral of degrees. Presumably, one is free of the need of further education when the final degree is at last received. Educators release the graduating class with ennobling speeches about a life of learning. But few teachers or professors feel disappointed if their students return after twenty years still repeating the opinions with which they had sent them in the world.

The interpenetration of schools and the community would naturally create opportunities for continuing education for everyone. More important, people might feel the need to read books, to talk to one another on matters of significance, occasionally even to enroll in a refresher course. But enrollment in courses is the least significant way in which education would occur. The primary means of perpetual learning would be the presence of ideas in the common world; the stimulus for it would come from the sense of excitement this presence creates. Our ultimate hope must reside in the development of habits of reflection. Only if we learn to think of life itself as a learning process, can we convince ourselves that thought makes a difference to existence, that our problems may be resolved by an understanding of our condition and commitments.

The creative unification of theory and practice would also eliminate the artificial line we draw between the months in which students learn and the months during which they are "on vacation." Presumably, we do not expect them to learn when they have

139

fun, nor to have fun while they are learning. If schooling could be focused on the rationalization of daily life, education would naturally go on throughout the year. There would be no need for a long vacation, nor any desire for one on the part of students. No child wants to take a break from enjoyable play; changes of topics and instruments can keep learning continuously vital and pleasant.

It is important to have natural breaks in one's life, special happenings which diversify the year. These could be introduced by relying on the seasons nature provides. The spring and the summer might be times at which children focus on their study of zoology and botany. This can be accompained by repeated visits to the country where city children, who otherwise never see animals breed and the wheat sprout, might actually become engaged in the process of growing food and tending the cattle we eat. There is great personal enrichment in having firsthand contact with the creative power of the earth which sustains us. It opens our eyes to the conditions of our being which a mediated world tends to obscure. It also gives us a sense of the mysterious creativity of our own bodies and souls, which is so natural that we have come to assume it without thanks. During the winter, by contrast, the focus might be on the city. Then the study of sociology and industrial psychology would naturally propel even country children into the brick jungles of the metropolis and into its factories.

Education conceived in this way would develop the body no less than the mind. Our current belief is that students have bodies primarily so they can keep them still. There are special hours reserved when tension can be relieved and energy released by violent motions directed at useless ends. Useful physical labor is treated with contempt by the educated classes, and this contempt is clearly reflected in the schools. Among the well-to-do, knowledge of practical physical skills is grounds for suspicion. It is the surest sign of humble origins. Educators find it difficult to believe that labor teaches us anything; they simply cannot see how it contributes to the education of the mind or even the development of character. Although many practitioners of the liberal arts take pleasure in watching organized sports, they view the football players in their classes as dumb oxen to be despised.

Mediation has created a world in which physical beauty is

achieved and aggression is displayed by others on our behalf. The models, the movie people, the Miss Americas are there for us to identify with them, for them to relieve us of the need to be beautiful or attractive. Organized sports in the stadium or on television are available for the relief of tension. A good brawl between hockey players on the ice engages us deeply; as our muscles vibrate at the sight of such brute strength and boldness, we can overlook our stretched belly and our flabby arms. Many an educated man today is an ignoramus when it comes to physical skills and an irresponsible guardian of his body.

If education is to overcome the worst effects of mediation, it must teach us a new attitude toward our bodies. We must learn neither to neglect them nor to worship them for the pleasant sights they provide. Bodies are centers of swirling activity: to educate them is to teach them new skills, and better ways to do well what they like to do. Physical exertion is perhaps the most immediate source of pleasure open to us. The skills of controlling our body and working with it are the first we learn: they are the foundation of our pride and self-esteem. The state of our physique is intimately tied to how we feel and what we think. And the view we take of our body determines what we think is natural. Without a healthy measure of identification with our physical self, we necessarily feel that we are strangers in the world.

Education must, then, be the development of body, intellect and character all at once. Abstract understanding should function as a beam of light that helps us learn physical skills and illuminates why they are necessary for health and self-respect. Physical operations, on the other hand, always serve as beautiful illustrations of abstract principles. They render intellectual beliefs vivid. By their intense natural reality, they strike down the pretensions of words and of the imagination.

All of this points in the end to the development of human character. John Stuart Mill was one of the very few modern thinkers who realized the immense importance of character for human welfare. He was right that freedom is an indispensable condition of the growth of character: in the end, we can accept and enjoy only those activities and that personality which we choose for ourselves. But what Mill overlooked was the impoverishment of choice and the distortion of character that come of truncated experience. In the mediated world much of what we ought to know and almost everything whose impact we must feel is inaccessible to us. As a result, there is little material for choice. Alternate lifestyles are difficult to conceive and impossible to flesh out. Divergent perspectives seem alien and lack validity.

Our activities are interlinked in a mediated system. Yet we operate in psychic isolation from one another. Our ignorance of the perspectives and circumstances of others makes them suspect in our eyes. Blacks, bankers, orientals, Catholics, southern rednecks, bleeding-heart liberals, the dumb Irish and the despicable Jews then become abstract stereotypes, caricatures born in ignorance to serve as objects of scorn. Nothing abstract can destroy these haunting images; our distance from the people so categorized and the frustrations native to a drifting world revitalize them at every turn. What our educational system must provide is immediate contact with persons of divergent backgrounds, convictions and social class. The stereotype that focuses our hatred is slowly destroyed as we meet the real people we lumped into a group. Suspicion is allayed when we look the other in the eye and see that he, too, is a human being with problems and hopes like ours.

Here again we find a demostration that there is a direct hookup between our senses and our feelings. Immediate contact with another human being, perception of his worries and his plight speak to us directly and with force. The impact can be increased by sustained exposure not only to the person and his thought but to his activities and his way of life. Part of the lifelong, practical, omnimodal education I am describing must focus on just such involvement of students with the diverse elements of the community. The children of the rich should be taught more than merely verbal appreciation of the glory of work. They must be given the opportunity to live with and learn to like working persons. There is no other way for anyone to understand the peculiar limits of the vision of laborers or the full meaning of a Friday night. The point of such exposure is not just that the rich student can then grow into a more understanding employer. To be more understanding is also to be ready to change existing structures in order to make them more humane.

The unmediated presence of person to person in a living community may well be expensive in terms of effort. But it has value both as means and end. As means, it serves to enrich the individual and to humanize his vision of the world. As end, it is a part of what fulfills human existence: the concerned companionship of persons. The shared joys and shared understanding that flow from such encounters may well be the meaning and in the end the fruition of the lives of most of us. A community that spends a substantial portion of its resources on the development of such widespread communication has itself as its greatest product. It may seem to some that such a society would be too narcissistic or too exclusively occupied with itself. But a moment's reflection should suffice to convince us that there is no aim more worthy than this for any society. External achievements, fine roads, great wealth, the pyramids themselves, are insignificant by comparison. If a society can find fulfillment only in the cold objects it creates or in the pursuit of posthumous fame, it will never find fulfillment at all. The prime task is to grow and flower like a rose. Social existence can also become an activity that is its own end; when it does it needs no justification beyond the beauty and the harmony it displays.

The democratic process and the educational process coincide in their aims. Both focus on the development of personality and through that on the intelligent self-determination of the community. The ultimate good that motivates both lies ready at hand, yet buried, in the human material with which they deal. Neither admits a higher perfection than can be achieved by having each individual live out his or her life as a satisfied, fully human member of a just community.

Viewed in this light, a large part of the governmental process itself becomes educational. Psychic distance between the government and the governed is sharply reduced by openness and fairness in the conduct of the public's business. But government officials and legislators must go beyond routine adherence to open and just policies or adherence to them for the sake of self-interest. They must reconceive the task of governing in terms of an interactive educational procedure. The task of the legislature is to educate the public by means of laws. But the legislators themselves must be educated in the needs and divergent purposes of the community at large. Our leaders must be our teachers; but in teaching us they must not suppose themselves educated or wise. No teacher is worth the pay he gets, no matter how little, if he makes it impossible for his students to teach him. President and Congress must come to the people to learn what must be. Their function is to recognize and formulate what we half-consciously desire or inarticulately demand.

The task of governing is so difficult because it requires the wisdom to educate, as well as the self-control to avoid rule by force. Paternalism in government is a deadly flaw. Yet to call the unwillingness to allow citizens to make their own mistakes "paternalism" is to introduce a mistaken idea of paternity. The relations of parent to child, government to the governed, teacher to student are all educational. They presuppose the readiness to learn on both sides. This must be grounded in mutual respect, in the desire to grow together and, most important of all, in the commitment to have each person retain the freedom to think and choose and feel for himself. Such freedom is not without limits. But in the vast majority of our choices we must view one another as mature adults, even if only as an attempt to create a self-fulfilling prophecy.

The educational process I have described tends to reduce or eliminate psychic distance. By a full exposure of each individual to nature and the community in which he lives, we can help him understand the conditions of his existence. By sustained experience of varied activities and results, we can get him to appreciate the distant and hidden consequences of his actions. By a broad acquaintance with our mediated chains, we can contribute to his grasp of the interconnectedness of things and to his feel and comprehension of his own place in the total system. By providing extensive personal contact with individuals different from him, we can promote the breakdown of racial, class, religious and other barriers between people. In these ways, we can slowly remove suspicion, hatred and the sense of impotence, all of which tend to immobilize our better human functions.

It is too costly or impossible to eliminate psychic distance by rejecting the mediated world. Nor can we look for immediacy to come to us by flipping a switch or swallowing a pill. Our aim must be to achieve immediacy by systematic labor. The mediated world is not so complex as to outstrip the mind. It is not so diverse as to make acquaintance with all or many of its types impossible. We can experience it and thereby make it our own. As we achieve immediacy in each sphere, our horizon broadens, our appreciation increases, our understanding is vitalized. As a result, we find it increasingly easier to appropriate the world, our society and our own acts. We then no longer seek to avoid responsibility for what we do. We mobilize to improve the world and ourselves. We begin to act like human beings who refuse to allow unavoidable mediation to keep them from being whole.